2-8-72

THE
HUMAN
METAPHOR

ELIZABETH SEWELL

THE
HUMAN
METAPHOR

UNIVERSITY OF NOTRE DAME PRESS

LIBRARY OF CONGRESS CATALOG CARD NUMBER: 63-19328

MANUFACTURED IN THE UNITED STATES OF AMERICA

1640666

METHOD

The rule, we find,
Is to be permeable; marbles stain;
Light filters through packed crystals; someone's pain
   Threads our interstices.
     Creatures of all kind
Are porous, breathe, fuse with their media;
   Closures but seem.
     Given a mind,
Much more so; tides of the universe have play;
Stars sift across our system once a day;
   Cosmos and chaos all we do.
     Then, Soul, defined
As other, yet materially fleshed,
Thy proper form retaining, o be meshed—
   What flood of love, air, fire,
Weep if thou will for shame and for desire,
   Shall stream thee through.

Foreword

IT IS WITH MUCH GRATITUDE THAT I ACKNOWLEDGE THE kindness of the English Department of Notre Dame University in asking me to give the lectures on which this book is based; and the kindness of the students in their response to them. I should like also to thank the Department of English of Los Angeles State College, the generous terms of whose Visiting Professorship made the writing of this possible.

My grateful thanks are also due to the following, for permission to quote from material of which they hold the copyright: The Center for the Study of Democratic Institutions, The Fund for the Republic, Santa Barbara, California, in respect of extracts from *Rediscovering Natural Law* by Scott Buchanan; the University of California Press in respect of extracts from *Annotated Index to the Cantos of Ezra Pound* by J. H. Edwards and W. W. Vasse; Hogarth Press, Ltd., London, in respect of material from *The Standard Edition of the Complete Psychological Works of Sigmund Freud,* Vols. XII, XVIII, XIX, XXI, this permission covering the world in the English language excluding the United States—and in the United States for this same material, to Basic Books, Inc., New York, in regard to extracts from "The Theme of the Three Caskets," *Collected Papers,* Vol. IV; to Liveright Publishing Corporation, New York, in respect of extracts from *Beyond the Pleasure Principle;* and to W. W. Norton & Co. Inc.,

7

in respect of quotations from *The Ego and the Id and Civilization and its Discontents*. Further, to Alfred A. Knopf, Inc., New York, in respect of extracts from the collection, *Essays,* by Thomas Mann; to Harcourt, Brace & World, Inc., in respect of the extract from *The City in History* by Lewis Mumford; to Cambridge University Press in respect of the extracts from *Science and Civilisation in China,* Vols. I, II and III, by Joseph Needham; and, finally, to New Directions in respect of quotations from the Cantos of Ezra Pound.

Contents

Prologue

THIS ESSAY, WHICH IN THE FULL SENSE OF THE WORD IS what this book is, has certain aims and makes certain assumptions. The two, as in all speculative work, are not easily distinguishable from one another: what you take for granted is also what you are looking for.

Its aim is to inquire into metaphor as one of the vital and basic powers of human thinking, a power which works by means of a constant play in which the mind singles out and matches figures, perceived, invented and inherited. It assumes that all thought works in some such fashion, not merely, despite their traditional association with figure and metaphor, the thought of poets. No doubt that poets are deeply concerned with this mode of thinking, partly as a result of their special instrument of language; but as a power of thinking it goes far beyond the limits of any one discipline.

Human thought is not merely metaphoric in operation. Itself forms one term of a metaphor. The other term may consist of the cosmic universe, or any detail within it, or may reach out beyond this, in exploration. With his unique figure of conscious mind-body, man is part of the total situation in which he thinks. That is, thought is never, despite appearances, a detached activity or product of the brain nor even a sole and pure relation between intellect and phenomena. It is always also involved with man's living self as a whole, and in its turn is a constituent element in man's continuous self-construction, be it individual or communal, at any given time and place.

We shall look at our own time and place from this point of view, to see how our methods of thought and our image of man are faring in their mutual and necessary interaction, this assessment to take the form largely of examining the metaphors which govern our thought nowadays, whether we are conscious of them or not. Finding both metaphors and methods only partial, as we shall do, we are going to turn to a long, resplendent, yet at present almost wholly overlooked tradition composed largely though not exclusively of poets, who speak to us of another method of thought. In this other method we are required, consciously and in confidence of our powers of interpretation, to think with the whole self. This includes using the figure of man, mind and body, as part of the metaphor and method. It also includes the similar use of the specifically human forms of living experience—love, suffering, the consciousness of failure or of mortality, for example—as metaphors, with power of interpretation beyond themselves which is one of the characteristics of metaphor or, in this its more extended form, of myth and allegory.

The alternative form of thinking which is put forward here, not in opposition but complement to the analytic and mathematical forms now prevailing, is no more than a restatement—Blake would call it an awakening, Bacon an instauration—of a persistent theme, relevant always but especially so today, when our ignoring and denial of the metaphoric relations between thought, universe and man have brought us to distortion and near-starvation. The poets point out to us this other possibility: to be human and to use our human being to think with. The fact that to call any thinking "anthropomorphic" nowadays is to insult it gives a measure of what has overtaken us, and of our need. Animals can operate intelligently, computers can compute, but to figure with the living self in the power of metaphor is the specific prerogative and unique potential of human beings.

THE
HUMAN
METAPHOR

One

MAN AND METHOD

I

"AS A MAN THINKETH, SO IS HE." IT IS AN OLD DRY NUT of a saying; but hold it in the hand [or mind], turn it over, warm it a little, and it begins to come to life. As we think, which is Method, and what we are, which is Man, stand in an "as-and-so" relation to one another, a relation of resemblance and of cause and effect.

Perhaps this relation between thinking and being, how we think and what we are, turns dull and opaque on us because we misconceive of each. We tend to regard each as a kind of state, or skill, which has to be acquired but which, once learned, can then be practised, on and on, like swimming or cookery. Our system of education fosters this misconception, with its current talk of "teaching students to think" or of "education for living." Neither can be learned or practised in this way since neither offers a fixed level of achievement, familiar once attained and thereafter mainly repetitive. The point about human thinking and human being, Man and Method in their intimate connection, is that they have to be made all the time. Each is a making.

To take Man first, the work of being human begins with the individual, as soon as he is born, and lasts lifelong. It is the main occupation, and travail, of our earlier years, but it never ceases as long as we are alive. (Of course a lot of people walking about are dead, as Ibsen so marvellously and continually warns us.) We have to work at ourselves, and other people work at or on us: our family, our teachers, our friends, the society to which we belong, our civil, cultural and ecclesiastical polity. We work at and on them too. The whole human world, individual and communal, is a constant making, a process of self-construction as Coleridge calls the human intelligence, an artifact as Vico so confidently proclaims human history to be—*che questo mondo civile egli certamente è stato fatto dagli uomini*—as it runs in the *Scienza Nuova*.

If we grasp this, we shall understand better how our Method, or way of thought, shapes the figure of Man, as part of this constant work going on. Method, too, has continually to be made and worked at. Conservation and renewal of our ways of thinking are part of the human corporate work obligatory on us all. Without doubt, however, much of the work here, upon Method itself, is carried on by certain particular individuals among us. I need a name for them, generically, and am going to call them dynasties, a metaphor helpful in suggesting linked successions of men with native power, with an inheritance, and with considerable command over us. (This can be seen most clearly when one of their number—Bacon, Galileo, Karl Marx—undertakes a major transformation of Method, for there ensues from it also a transformation in Man's image of himself.) Such beings resemble dynasties also in that they often have minor but numerous retinue, who battle among themselves. Let us consider them, in these terms, for a moment, for they are important to us here, providing us with one of our main sources of material and counsel.

As Western civilization has grown up, seven great dynasties of men have grown up with it, bringing forward from the past their special calling with its living tradition, working actively at it in the present and shaping their own age thereby, then handing it on to the future with an increment of power and growth. The seven are priests, artists of the non-linguistic arts, poets, governors, philosophers, scientists, historians. The first three, as far as we can tell, have been with us since the beginning, since man was man; the last four make an appearance slightly later, though still from very early times. What we call genius nearly always makes itself known to us under one of these forms, or more than one, for they are not species or categories and it is possible to combine them. (Where, for instance, should we put Goethe, or Marx, or Thomas Aquinas?) These are the royalty of the spirit. They produce, to take a sample, political systems, integral calculus, tragic drama, fugue, new approaches to God, nuclear fission. Simultaneously with all of these, however, and in and through them, they work at Method, at extending the ways and power of human thought. Thus they work at Man. They work at us.

Between us all, "this world which is each man's work," in Dylan Thomas's admirably traditional phrase, gets fashioned. Part of that making is the reciprocal influence of our methods of thought and our image of man. How we think, to return to our starting-point, determines what we think we are.

We are uneasy at present about how we are. Accepting and sharing that discomfort, we in this study are going to look at its nature as best we can, and see how far it does in fact connect with our present ways of thinking. After that, we can go on to ponder what changes, and ameliorations, in our thinking may be open to us. For what is made can always be remade, as the promises attest —et renovabis faciem terrae. As for our own method here, we shall, as is proper to my trade of poetry, avail ourselves of the great tradition residing in those who belong to the dynasties, past and present. In addition, I mean to work with two other resources which seem to poets reliable. One is the use of figure and metaphor, the selection and combination of images as signs by which to read what is going on. The other is personal experience. Out of these three—inheritance, figuring, the immediately known and lived—this study will in its turn have to be made.

II

Uncovering our state of mind today can be accomplished, short of the sociological survey, only by means of hints and indications.

We will start, in our attempt at self-discovery relating to Man and Method, with an object which is also an image, and then go on to a restricted group of people whose characteristics I can describe, and see what we can draw from both.

The object in question used to be, and possibly still is, part of the official furniture of any office belonging to one particular manufacturing corporation in the United States. The organization, already of mammoth size and still expanding, manufactures and markets computers or, as we tend to call them, electronic brains. On the wall of the office or on the desk of each highly-trained representative, at the heart as it were of technological progress and confronting technician and machine alike, the company posted a little white card. It said, simply, THINK. We had better accept the invitation.

Taking this at its face value to start with, we may ask what the admonition implies. We can judge fairly reliably what kind of thought is meant. It must be the kind appropriate to the scientific and technological situation. The card appears as an exhortation to carry forward the great tradition of Western scientific method, of which both man and machine in this office may be regarded as end-products. It epitomizes that tradition and can send us back to its beginnings, to the seventeenth century and, specifically, Descartes from whom we trace this modern method of ours, the Descartes of the *Discours de la Méthode* and of the *Cogito ergo sum,* a Method and a view of Man. We will think about the method first.

It has become very plain and vastly developed in the three hundred years since Descartes' time. The grand Cartesian doubt, which is a working conviction held on principle, asserts that all that we know by the senses, including ourselves, may be illusory and is certainly suspect. The mind can rely only on what the mind makes, and its most reliable construct is mathematics. By applying this instrument to the external world, the mind can counteract the hypothetical unreliability of that world because in the process "all real relations are dissolved into logical relations between man-made symbols." (I am quoting from Chapter VI of *The Human Condition* by Hannah Arendt, which we shall discuss shortly.) Notice that this process excludes language, the relations in which are not and can never be solely logical. The method, totally impersonal because designed to be universally valid, operates through instruments, mental or technological and in either case mathematical, of ever-increasing power and complexity, which have been devised in order to interpret the material universe into the terms of the mental method and so render the former subject to the latter, both in theory and practice. We should notice, before we go on to other things, two consequences of this method. One is that the universe, as we are required to conceive of it, has become vaporized, so to speak, into expanding process, dynamic configurations of energy, and sets of relations. The other is the proliferation of technology and its products; the monstrously marvellous and numerous machines.

This is all spread over three hundred years. Within the last twenty of them, however, the method has reached what appears to us all as a kind of climacteric. It has invited to earth the blazing power latent in the atom but hitherto, in its explosive state, quarantined in a sun or a star; and it has sent out the first structures, and men with them, away from the earth into the universe at large. Poised on the edge of limitless expanses, in touch with sources of energy which seem infinite, this method of Descartes and of modern science is prospering exceedingly. Now what about the counterpart of Method, which is Man? Is he prospering in this situation and tradition which THINK symbolizes, and does his state exemplify the view of Man implicit in the Cartesian method from the beginning?

It is possible to make certain general statements about the condition of human beings in our present world, but they all have the disadvantage of being generalities and nothing more. So, for a characterization of our time, I am going to turn to a group whom I know fairly well and describe their characteristics as I have observed them. These are college students, men and women, white and Negro, in the United States. No group can be fully representative; parts cannot be wholes. But I prefer partiality based on firsthand experience to general statements which are not, and there are factors in this group which make it a reasonable choice. Students in America are mixed and numerous enough to form at least some sort of sample of the population, and the United States is mixed and numerous enough to have affinities with the world outside of itself.

The first point in my description might seem surprising, because there exists a stereotyped opinion that Americans are materialistic. One of the most striking things about American students is the degree of abstractness in their thinking and writing. They talk, readily and fluently, like would-be philosophers, metaphysicians, theoretical psychologists or sociologists, civil servants, academic pedants, like anything in fact except what they are, active young mind-body organisms in a perceptible world. It takes work and time to get them to write and think concretely, to notice the world around them with their senses, to observe fact; to come down to earth instead of being up in a cloud of hot air. Their bodies lead an active life but usually entirely detached from that of the mind. They have little confidence in their powers of imagination. It is as if some middle term in a progression or a system of communication with the real world were missing or lost.

There is also in them, as I see it, an uncertain hovering between hunger and fear, uncertainty about where to attach and apply these two basic, and good, instincts. There is a widespread hunger, almost frightening in its intensity since it suggests something akin to starvation, for what in an old phrase was called "newness of life." Any teacher or thinker, for example, who has a fresh approach to his subject and to our general problems, some vitality and something personal and genuine to offer, will find among the student body in America a welcome and response he would not find in England, perhaps not anywhere else. Again, this runs counter to the stereotype that Americans are conventional and conformist. Certainly the classroom in the United States can be almost disconcertingly experimental. Yet there is conformism too, and this is where the fear comes in. With the hunger for new life and activity is a fear of newness, of tampering with the status quo, of anything which might alter "the American way of life." The change into something really different, which is so disturbing and precious a quality of life and activity, is precluded by fear at this point.

Under this fear, any innovation becomes destructive and any eccentricity a threat to the over-all norm. The notion of selfhood in America of course entails the right to change—every living thing changes all the time, naturally. It does not, however, entail the right to change the *ideal* of the individual. This ideal we must all strive to resemble, and all individual change has to be directed to that end. Prolonged and deliberate divergence from the ideal is a violation of the agreement to regulate change in this way. (How the ideal is arrived at would make an interesting study but does not concern us directly here.) In so far as American students are conformist, they are so under the influence of nationally distributed ideals, desiring not so much to resemble one another as to resemble the accepted type.

Politically, fear of radical change in the future means that American selfhood at the national level has come to be identified with a present and a past. It is as if a whole dimension of time had been dropped out by agreement, and the succession now went: Past—Present—Eternity. If this is how one sees the political situation, any attempt to change the status quo at all profoundly is menacing; it is more, it is treasonable. From the fear at this level springs the success, among a considerable number of American students today, of certain ultraconservative political movements.

To speak of fear of change, or resistance to the idea of change, with regard to America seems in a way nonsensical. Compared with many another society, American life gives the appearance of changing all the time. Do not Americans change, often with a dizzy speed, whole blocks of their cities' architecture, their private domiciles, their automobiles, their styles in clothing and interior decoration, their stock-market holdings, their slimming diets, their husbands and wives? This, up to a point, is true. On a closer look, however, this seems to be much less change than substitution. There is a wide freedom for change provided that "plus ça change, plus c'est la même chose." Go on changing, but into the same thing every time and for ever and ever.

And now, fear may enter in earnest; for this is a nightmare. Or, to put it another way, it is a system operating as a machine, where the human being implicated in the system has neither control over its compulsive monotony nor freedom to emerge. Fear enters, and hunger, again here for American students. There are those who hanker after just such regularity and predictability (they will probably call it security) and such people may enter careers that appear to offer this, in the great manufacturing corporations for instance, and then become machines so effectively that their employers find it necessary to give their middle-aged executives re-education courses in mental initiative, creative thinking, or, simply, the humanities. There is another group, however, whose hunger will take them the other way, who are hungry to be free of the machine at any cost, yet do not know how. Students who feel like this will be suspicious of all authority and of nearly everything that is officially offered them. Their continual restlessness gets them into trouble with their parents and instructors; their occasional but by no means exceptional lawlessness may get them into trouble with the police.

At this point we move outside America. A good deal of what I have described is probably not peculiar to the United States, but this certainly is not. Young people all over the world appear to be feeling and behaving in this way, moved by fear at being caught in something that has become machine-like, and by hunger to be out of that and into something else, even if only into the unknown. They died in the streets of Budapest for this eight years ago, but it transcends our present political divisions. Even the new countries who are at present making their way, politically and technologically, in the world will not be clear of it for long. If our information is correct, both the Soviet Union and India show signs of this hunger and fear among their young people too.

Whatever else this restless stirring all over the world may mean, it does suggest that our state today tends to have similar features everywhere. Yet this stirring is not to be thought of as purely negative, at least to judge by American students again. It does spring in part from fear at being trapped in the dead and the machine-like, but also, much more, from hunger—to rejoice in the new age so plainly upon us and in man's unparalleled achievements in thought and the technological embodiments of that thinking. A year or two ago, one of my Negro students in the American South wrote an imaginative piece for me, half vision, half poem, sharing with Major Gagarin his experience which none of us had had before, the passion of exhilaration and awe at being out beyond the curve of the world, the pride in this communal deed, the sheer beauty, seen for the first time, of what the seer had imagined a century earlier, with no less passion: "O vast Rondure, swimming in space, Covered all over with visible power and beauty . . . the manifold grass and waters . . . and countless stars above." Reading her paper I recognized my own delight of a year earlier, a common experience I am certain, at hearing, in England as I then was, the voice of that first sputnik of ours up there among the moons and spaces. We hunger to be "we"; yet we fear too.

Now, to pull our findings together if we can: we (if this group, young, thinking, *engagé*, yet ordinary in the best sense, may stand as "we") show signs of having lost some middle ground, some communicating system between our thoughts, which we express with increasing abstraction, and what might be called our ecological habitat, i.e., our bodies first, our setting in the natural world, and the company of our fellow-men. This lack of something in the middle induces a condition of fear and hunger relating, sometimes ambivalently, to organic change as against machine-like automatism, and to commitment on a wide scale to human being and human community.

Something may strike us about this. Our state, combining however uneasily abstraction and automatism, closely resembles the actual Cartesian method itself: mathematics and machines. It suggests that Method and Man do in fact stand in a metaphoric relation to one another. As we think, so we become. We must go back to THINK and to its seventeenth century origins, the *Cogito ergo sum*, if we are to understand this better.

We took THINK, when we began on it, at its face value. The little card looks down on both man and machine: is it then addressed to both? Or might it be not a verb but a noun, classifying the contents of the premises? The machine is a think, man is a think too. This is not whimsy nor an attempt at humour. It is only putting *Cogito ergo sum* in a slightly less hackneyed way. We need to think about that dictum of one of the founders of the scientific method. To do this we will set alongside it another saying, equally well-known and well-worn so that they start fair, spoken by a scientist from the same crucial century, and equally having to do with man and thinking. The dynasties are about their work here. Descartes belongs in two of them, as scientist and philosopher. This other is scientist and philosopher also, but has claims to two other dynasties as well, for he has some touch of the priest, in the widest sense of the word, and some of the poet, which shows itself in the saying of his we are going to look at. This other, as you may have surmised, is Pascal.

Pascal, like Descartes, has something to say about man and thinking. He says it in the form of a metaphor. "Man is a reed," he says; then adds, "but a reed that thinks." Where Descartes casts his saying in the form of premise and deduction or, say, a proposition in symbolic logic—I think, therefore I am; if P, then Q—Pascal leaps into metaphor or poetry. He does not indicate that there are points of analogy between the two phenomena or images he has chosen. He comes out with the kind of non-sense a poet uses. Man *is* a reed; the reed thinks.

The metaphor is a pregnant one. We are simultaneously to be humbled and exalted. There is nothing glorious in being a reed. It is a fragile thing, easily snapped, soon rotted, one amongst innumerable specimens like itself. It has been thought glorious to be a man, to be human. (Somehow one feels impelled to put that in the past tense.) The true sense of man's glory, however, or even of human worth, to put it in a lower key, was never an overweening arrogance. That is the Greek *hubris,* leading only to disaster, the theme that tragedy deals so faithfully with. We have always in our right minds known ourselves flawed, finite, and shockingly vulnerable, so that our sense of reality convinces us that man's was always a "wounded splendour," in that notable theological formula. We assent then, in some sort, to this half of Pascal's statement. Yet he goes on to say that the reed thinks, and though the whole cosmos should fall in utter ruin and destruction on the reed and crush it, the reed would nevertheless be greater than the sum of things which destroyed it, because it would know what was happening. Thought here is consciousness or self-consciouness. The self-conscious reed is Pascal's image of Method and Man.

It is metaphor, that is clear, and a moment ago we said that Descartes' formulation was not. Yet when you begin to look at the latter's pronouncement more closely, does it not too begin to show signs of being a metaphor, a ghost of a metaphor at least? It is Pascal's metaphor but with the middle term removed. Pascal

says, "L'homme n'est qu'un roseau, mais c'est un roseau pensant."
Descartes says, *Cogito ergo sum*, "L'homme n'est qu'un . . . pensant":—Man is a . . . thinking. After three centuries of this comes
the little white card in the business office, which says in its turn,
"Man is a think is a machine."

A middle term has gone, just as a middle term seemed to be
lacking when we looked at our state of mind in this present age.
That middle term is the conscious use of metaphor which admits
the phenomenal world, in relation to thought and to man, as a
means of thinking. It is not metaphor itself that is suppressed. In
this respect we have much misunderstood the nature of Method in
general, encouraged in our misunderstanding by many within the
Cartesian method itself, as we shall see in a while. The metaphoric
relation between Method and Man holds, and holds now. It is in-
destructible. Yet because there is no conscious relation to, or use
of, metaphor, we are delivered to the hidden rather than the overt.
The metaphor remains, the fusion of the I with depersonalized
mathematical abstractions of the scientific method which embody
themselves in machines. Our fears and hungers, our sense of a lost
term in communication, testify to the fact that we dimly recognize
the metaphor, of Method and Man, for what it is, and credit it with
the power metaphors have. That is why it frightens us, the more
so since we have learned no skill in this type of thought, nor even
to pay attention to it.

At present we will not go further than this loss of a middle term,
in Method and in Man. We have glimpsed that it has to do with the
conscious use of metaphor and the admission, as part of the method
of thought, of the phenomenal world, but we need to learn more
about the loss, the gap, if we can. To this end we will look now at
three books, all of which have appeared within the last few years,
which address themselves to this problem.

III

The Phenomenon of Man by Teilhard de Chardin first appeared
in the French edition in 1955; *Personal Knowledge* by Michael Po-

lanyi in 1958; *The Human Condition* by Hannah Arendt in 1958 also.[1] The titles of these works, set side by side like that, have a certain significance of their own: man, humanity, the person. They are all, among other things, works on Method, and the fact that they should appear within so short a space of time is perhaps an indication of the urgency of the problems we face in relation to Man and Method at the present.

The first of the three is the most controversial. The pattern of attacks and defences which have gathered round it, the ecclesiastical cautions in its regard, its surprising popular success, need not be dwelt on here—they are common knowledge. When all this has died down, it seems to me that the lasting value of the book, besides being a marker of an enormous and widespread hunger among educated people for a kind of cosmic metaphysic, may be seen to be methodological. At any rate, it is from this point of view that I want to discuss it here. The centre of Teilhard de Chardin's view is man, the sentient, thinking, conscious phenomenon and the living soul. The writer's frame is the great formative work going on in this planet; formation of the globe itself first of all, then of living things of all kinds, then of man. His approach is unlike the prevailing scientific view in two ways: first, he postulates an "inwardness" to matter from the beginning, since the increasing inwardness of living things and, eventually, of human consciousness, was to emerge from it; second, he incorporates mind, the powers of thought of the human phenomenon, fully into his over-all view, mind not secularised back into some rigidly materialistic or determined universe or else ignored altogether as an epiphenomenon outside the biologist's proper sphere, but human thinking seen in a continuity from the purely physical forms into the mental ones and thence into the great social forms of man's thought, society, organization, technology. The human being is here restored to solidarity with the living, growing, orderly current of power which evolution is and by which we move into the future, human intelligence appearing both as the spearhead of direction of evolutionary forces and also as the living and perpetually self-renewing epitome

[1] The first was published by Editions du Seuil, Paris, the second and third by the University of Chicago Press.

of the method of the whole process, the kind of "inspired groping" which can produce new forms, in life physical or life mental or social.

Michael Polanyi is concerned with how the human mind knows what it knows, how it learns, how it thinks. Particularly he examines the premises and foundations of thought in science, his own discipline, and the so-called scientific method. He, too, is thinking about the emergence of man, and hence of mind in evolution, and it is the inadequacy or failure of current scientific theory to account for this which ushers in his whole discussion. With meticulous logic he shows that the theory that the different living species have come into existence solely through chance mutations has to co-exist in our minds with our simultaneous belief that we, as human beings, are capable of recognizing and appraising order (among living beings as elsewhere) when we see it, and also the belief that no highly significant order can ever be solely due to purely random occurrences but must depend on the operation of some ordering principle. We accomplish this feat of self-contradiction, he says, by keeping these last two beliefs at the back of our minds but out of sight, and attending only to the accepted scientific theory. This pattern of behavior permeates the whole of science today. "A scientist can accept, therefore, the most inadequate and misleading formulation of his own scientific principles without ever realizing what is being said, for he automatically supplements it by his tacit knowledge of what science really is, and thus makes the formulation ring true."

The "logical muddle" inherent in contemporary evolutionary theory is, the writer says, "a piece of equivocation, unconsciously prompted by the urge to avoid facing the problem set by the fact that the universe has given birth to these curious beings, including people like ourselves." The more general yet similar discrepancy between the official version of what scientific method is and what really goes on in the living discipline, "this immense power of self-deception," is due to the modern mind's "paramount desire for impersonal knowledge." This kind of thinking (which is of course the Cartesian kind) does not want, so Michael Polanyi says, to account for the presence of man in the universe nor to have knowledge root in the fact of being a man. "The great movement for independent thought instilled in the modern mind a desperate refusal of all knowledge that is not absolutely impersonal, and this implied in its turn a mechanical conception of men which was bound to deny man's capacity for independent thought."

To save us from this compulsion, from Man-is-a-think-is-a-machine, Michael Polanyi directs our attention to epistemology, to how man thinks, learns, knows. We shall find here, too, a situation analogous to that which he was considering in the beginning, human minds attending consciously to some activity in the foreground of their awareness, but supplementing and subtending this all the time, unconsciously, with beliefs or unarticulated activity held in the background of the mind but not focally attended to. Michael Polanyi calls this last capacity of ours the tacit coefficient or tacit component of all our knowledge.

He begins this part of his enquiry by talking first about skills. These may be bodily, i.e., muscular, or intellectual, and our powers here are continuous with those of animals confronting challenges in their physical or "mental" worlds. In either case he notes a peculiar feature of a skilled performance of any kind: it depends on the observance of a set of rules which are not known, as such, by the organism following them. We focus on the aim of the performance, not on the rules, but we are aware of these or we could not accomplish our aim. As the next step, he considers the use of tools. For anything to be capable of being used by us as a tool, we have to identify it as a tool and to believe that it can be used for that particular purpose, and that we can so use it. Yet, similarly, when we begin using tools we do not focus on them but on our aim or problem; and here Michael Polanyi comes up with a wonderful suggestion—that we assimilate the tool as part of our own body and then proceed with the job in hand, while the tool-handling and the skill it requires accompany us as our body accompanies us but are not focally attended to. This is true of physical tools *and also* of intellectual ones. "We pour ourselves out into them and assimilate them as parts of our own existence . . . Hammers and probes can be replaced by intellectual tools; think of any interpretative framework and particularly of the formalism of the exact sciences." Our

instruments are extensions of ourselves as body and mind, never
the self-affirmation of man as mind alone as Descartes' *Cogito ergo
sum* proposes, nor an equating of man and think as his ghost-meta-
phor implies. They work solely because we lend them the living
pulsing activity of our own power to think, of which the body is an
integral part.

The human integrity is affirmed here, since all thought and
knowledge depend ultimately on the thinking individual commit-
ting himself, in lonely faith and responsibility, to his selected instruments and to his problem and aim, believing in and bringing
with him the "tacit component" of his thought with its roots in the
bodily activity and inarticulate exquisite skills of the human body.
Thought becomes once again an integral human activity, akin in its
"groping" (a term which Michael Polanyi shares with Teilhard de
Chardin) to the strivings of the lowliest organisms, and, like them,
aiming forward towards advance in the field—using that word in its
technical sense, as in the morphogenetic field of embryology—of
the evolution of all living things on this earth.

In *The Human Condition* Hannah Arendt invites us to look at
ourselves as human beings individual, social, and political, at the
point where we now are, the beginning of "a new and unknown
age" ushered in by the first atomic explosions and the first man-
made objects in outer space. She is concerned in this work, she
says, with activity, the kind of activity which is accessible to all
average human beings, and not, therefore, with thought as such.
It is true that throughout the book the author does not dwell on
the nature of thought, rather on its metamorphoses and effects in
history, for instance the interaction of philosophy and politics in
the classical world and of science and politics in the modern, or
the corresponding change in the assessment of the relative value
of action and contemplation. Yet in a way there is a paradox in this
avowal or disavowal of the work's intention, for the Prologue
where this is discussed invites us explicitly to think, to "think
what we are doing," claiming that thoughtlessness in all its forms
is one of the principal characteristics of our time; and the last few
pages of the remarkable final chapter return again to thought, seen
not as a function of the brain, which then electronic machines can

carry out far more effectively than we can, but as part of the human *vita activa*, perhaps the most active activity of them all. Thinking human beings, in this age, are not grown rarer; and "Thought, finally, . . . is still possible." How deeply the writer is in fact concerned with and committed to thought and thinking as such can be seen yet more plainly in her next book, the collection of essays entitled *Between Past and Future*, 1961. In the Preface she says, "Only insofar as he thinks . . . does man in the full actuality of his concrete being live in this gap between past and future." She adds, a little later, "The trouble, however, is that we seem to be neither equipped nor prepared for this activity of thinking, of settling down in the gap between past and future." She goes on to call her own essays exercises in political thought, and offers them to us on those terms.

In *The Human Condition*, the modern dilemma of thought is presented as world alienation in two forms, flight from earth into universe, and flight from earth into self. The first consists in taking the active centre of thinking, the Archimedean point from which all else is to be regarded, and setting it down, so to speak, outside the terrestrial frame of things, out in the universe. The second, Cartesian, consists in removing that same point of operation to within the self, the functioning mind being considered as alone directly knowable and certain. The trouble with the first is "that while man can *do* things from a 'universal,' absolute standpoint, . . . he has lost his capacity to *think* in universal, absolute terms . . . Instead of the old dichotomy between earth and sky we have a new one between man and the universe, or between the capacities of the human mind for understanding and the universal laws which man can discover and handle without true comprehension." The trouble with the second is that from it follows the implication that the patterns of our own minds are all we can ever know, and our perception of external reality, that is, the universe at large and all that is in it, is always only a mental construct which we make and then reperceive (as so much of modern physics does in fact suggest).

The processes of our own thought seem once more to have brought us to a state of imprisonment or paralysis in automatism.

Indeed Hannah Arendt says that process itself always tends towards an automatism which cannot but spell disaster for life on any fully human terms. Yet human beings, at the level of thought and action, have always at their disposal one resource, both simple and "miraculous" in the exact sense: the power to initiate action including the activity of thinking, to begin the new and improbable. This, like the power to think, is still possible, and it is this, as the writer re-emphasizes in *Between Past and Future,* which constitutes our freedom.

All these three works are of very considerable scope, and I have not come near to covering their full arguments, merely taken what was to our purpose here. Each in its own way speaks to the great centre of Man and Method, and to the gap which we surmise has opened in it in modern times. Teilhard de Chardin would save us from lonely underestimation of the human mind in the universe by having us see that very power of thought as of crucial and unique significance and purpose in the natural world among the works of God. Michael Polanyi would save us from dislocation from our instruments of power or idolatry of them by a new inquiry into, and affirmation of, human thought as mind and body, with faith and personal commitment as the foundation of all learning and knowing. Hannah Arendt would save us from self-generated automatism by offering us freedom in its essential form, the power to initiate new beginnings, in thought and action.

It is noticeable that in the attention they pay to the real dislocation of our time, none of the three is drawn into the pseudo-dislocations which are its minor and distracting results: the commonly accepted division between science and arts, for instance. It is the unity of the human endeavour which they put forward, that unity which we are calling Method and Man, the work of being human carried on by us all including our seven dynasties. Teilhard de Chardin traces the development in time of the forms, inanimate, then animate in rising complexity and levels of achievement, at length human. Through man and his mind and the forms which that mind makes possible come the next stages in this series, the human achievements such as society and politics and culture and technology, yet all in continuity. It is a vision matched in its unity only by

one other that I know: that of Ovid in the *Metamorphoses,* great
methodology as it is, which also traces the forming and reforming
of "plastic Nature," and makes an absolute continuity between natural history and human history, with, at the point of transformation, the figure of the poet, Orpheus. We are directed to language, as
the means above all by which man constructs himself and his characteristic forms of life and action.

In Michael Polanyi and Hannah Arendt, there is a similar, if
rather differently located, emphasis on unity. Thought, so the former affirms, is carried on in both art and science, and these activities are continuous with one another, not conflicting as in our modern inadequate view. What is more, language is here discussed as
an instrument of thought, less precise than mathematics, and for
that very reason better able to correspond with experience more
fully and to give greater play to the vital powers of inarticulate
judgment, which, well used, are of great speculative power. In
Hannah Arendt's work, art is again affirmed as a form of thinking—
"The immediate source of the art work is the human capacity for
thought"—and language comes to occupy supreme importance as
that which alone makes human society and politics possible in the
first place. One sentence in *The Human Condition,* in Chapter IV,
sticks—if one is a poet—in the memory. It says: "Of all the things
of thought, poetry is closest to thought."

Thought is what we are trying to think about here. These three
contemporary workers upon Man and Method direct us to look at
what is going on in art and language and poetry as well as at science,
that is, they send us abroad among the dynasties in their common
task. That middle term we seem to have lost, in thinking and living,
may reside somewhere here.

IV

We have been figuring Descartes' method, as against Pascal's,
by saying that the former dismisses the overt use of metaphor,
though it cannot dismiss its own metaphoric relation, as Method,
to Man, this now merely becoming hidden instead of open. To speak

of the dismissal of metaphor by scientists in the seventeenth century is not, however, merely figurative. The Royal Society, founded for the advancement of science in England in the 1660's, upheld such a dismissal, explicitly, as principle and policy. Away with the fictions of the poets, we find them saying; let our thoughts and speech be plain and matter-of-fact.

It must have seemed then simply the discarding of ancient lumber in favour of new instruments of power which would bring results. Not until the end of the eighteenth century did those results begin to be widely visible. By then they were becoming literally visible. Signs of industrial progress, factories and machines and products, were appearing everywhere, in England especially. Other results, however, were also becoming apparent by this time, the consequences of scientific method on man and society when the full energies of the whole culture are concentrated at that point. Particularly in England and Germany, the two countries which will lead the world in technological advance during the nineteenth century, warning voices begin to be heard. It is the poets who speak of danger. They are not bewailing the dismissal of metaphor as a method of thought from their own professional grounds, vital though it is to poetry. What they have to say is far more serious: that the denial of metaphor, with all that that implies, could mean that we are going to be maimed in our vitals.

The reason for this is that the loss of metaphor is the loss of language, and language is the essential instrument of the human imagination.

Western thought, through the tradition of its languages, has postulated some centre of the mind where we work in and through images: *imaginatio, Einbildung.* To this centre come all images of the external world and of the body given by our senses; by means of language which we superimpose on, or fuse with, them, we make sense of the universe and ourselves, and can also use the images, by virtue of the fact that words are not denotative symbols alone but clusters of allusive and metaphoric potential, for speculative construction. Metaphor is all the idiom of language untranslatable into a system of algebraic notation. By means of it we are enabled to think with, and not only about, both the universe and ourselves.

To dismiss metaphor, therefore, is to dismiss all this field for thought and to deny any value to this thinking. If you are going to commit yourself to logic as alone reliable, you will inevitably move out of words into meaningless symbols, out of language into mathematics. We know, from the history of science, to what an extent this has happened. What we did not know when we embarked on it was what the consequences in human terms might be.

The imagination is not merely the place where images are worked with. Simultaneously with this activity, and probably inseparably from it, we create in this centre the self-image, man's image of himself, body and mind. If you deny language to this faculty of the mind, you will half cripple it but you will not paralyze its creating of man's self-image. But the self-image appears to be affected by the method under which the mind is operating. Denied language, the mind will have to work now on what you are offering it instead. If this is logic and mathematics, it will try to build its human image out of that. If man cannot image himself through a word-speech into the universe which those words and his senses bring with them, he will begin to image himself into a think and a machine, which is what the Cartesian method offers. So a great voice begins to cry, in London. "They became what they beheld," it cries, over and over again. We were beholding, then as now, the ever-increasing power of scientific method; but for this poet, the results of that method as made visible in technology were not so much realities in themselves as master-images of what was happening within the minds of men. The poet is William Blake.

During his life he was obscure and unregarded and poor. Since his death we seem to have agreed to regard him as a great original, also, with tolerance, as a little mad, and to pay attention almost solely either to his shorter and easier works, the *Songs of Innocence and Experience* or *The Marriage of Heaven and Hell,* or to his drawings and prints, voided of their text. However, we do call his long verse narratives the Prophetic Books. In these he presents a cosmos of the imagination, at once inside and outside the mind, immense landscapes and starscapes, gulfs and wildernesses, celestial mills turning their wheels in the voids between the stars, huge continents and cities which are at once places in the imagination, "of which this present world is but a shadow," and Europe and

Asia and Africa and America and England and even the streets of London; all this topography is fused with the landscape and figures of the Bible, and is inhabited by powers, physical and mental, to whom Blake gives human shape, male or female—"my Giant Forms," he calls them. We are going to look at one of these Prophetic Books, *Jerusalem,* which he was working on between 1804 and 1820. In Blake's case that means not only composing the poetry, but also limning in line and colour the illustrations which accompany or enclose the pages of written text, and engraving and printing the work himself.

The poem faces us, first of all, with a scene of disaster. Something dreadful has happened, and the giant Albion (or England) who, for Blake, represents all mankind, is deathly sick. He lies like a pale corpse, the seas washing his hair, and his sickness has spread everywhere, "a mighty Polypus growing," the poet says, "From Albion over the whole Earth." In an evil night, "A dark and unknown night, indefinite, unmeasurable, without end," Albion sleeps a deadly sleep, the sleep of Ulro. Albion is mankind, sleeping himself into death, and only the poet sees this and must do what he can to save him:

I see the Past, Present and Future existing all at once
Before me. O Divine Spirit, sustain me on thy wings,
That I may awake Albion from his long and cold repose.

What is it that has drained Albion of his strength and beauty and left him a living corpse? We spoke earlier about a ghost or shadow in connection with Descartes and his metaphor. Here the ghost appears, for over Albion hovers his Spectre and it is this which has caused the sickness in mankind.

But the Spectre, like a hoar frost and a Mildew, rose over
    Albion,
Saying, "I am God, O Sons of Men! I am your Rational Power!
Am I not Bacon and Newton and Locke . . .
Who teach Doubt and Experiment . . . ?
Vain foolish Man, wilt thou believe without Experiment?
And build a World of Phantasy upon my Great Abyss?
                                        (Chapter 3)

In the course of the poem Blake drives home what he is saying here:

> . . . it is the Reasoning Power,
> An Abstract objecting power that Negatives everything;
> This is the Spectre of Man, the Holy Reasoning Power,
> And in its Holiness is closed the Abomination of Desolation.
>   (Chapter 1)

> The Spectre is the Reasoning Power in Man . . . when separated
> From Imagination and closing itself in steel as in a Ratio . . .
>   (Chapter 3)

Blake's Spectre, usurping the place and power of the living organism in its fulness, is unmistakably Cartesian method and modern science in its extreme phase; "Rational Philosophy and Mathematic Demonstration" is another of his epithets for it, identified by the great names in the Cartesian tradition and leading forward to the logical outcome of the process as we have seen it in our day. First, astonishing as it is that Blake saw it, this kind of thought will lead by its own inexorable mathematical logic to a universe of randomness: "And Accident and Chance were found hidden in Length and Bredth and Highth," as Blake puts it. Secondly it will, as he says, close itself in steel.

The method of thought, in Blake's vision, takes shape and is embodied in the machines which are its logical conclusion and extension of power, and which, as technology, spread out from England so mightily and so far.

> I turn my eyes to the Schools and Universities of Europe,
> And there behold the Loom of Locke, whose Woof rages dire,
> Wash'd by the Water-Wheels of Newton: black the cloth
> In heavy wreathes folds over every Nation: cruel Works
> Of many Wheels I view, wheel without wheel, with cogs tyrannic
> Moving by compulsion each other . . .
>   (Chapter 1)

The places of education and thought, of humane studies, have become mechanised factories, with the method itself going through the looms like cloth and fuelling the production line. It is a perfect imaging of "Man is a think is a machine" at one of the nerve-centres of our intellectual life. In what seems to modern readers an almost more extraordinary image, Blake says that "Bacon and Newton, sheath'd in dismal steel, their terrors hang / Like iron scourges over Albion." Think of an intercontinental ballistic missile with an atomic warhead, as a *kind of thinking* sheathed in steel impending over humanity, and you will see the force of this.

Meantime, and in these very terms, the mind of man must go on with its function of creating the image of the self and society. Blake uses technological metaphor for this process, calling it forging or weaving: "The Male is a furnace of beryl; the Female is a golden Loom." In the great city of the poem, Golgonooza which is Commerce and also London, this work goes on day and night. Yet because of the unbalance in the method and in the mind, the work goes awry and produces violence and war, lust and hate between the sexes, and a pseudo-religion which is founded not on faith and forgiveness but self-righteousness and morality. Blake casts his net very wide here, saying that the excess of think produces results right through the human fabric of society, in politics, in human relationships, in religion.

It is very important to be clear about what the poet is saying. He is not crying out against the scientific method or mathematical intelligence as such, only against the exclusive pursuit of it and the neglecting of all else. This idolatry of think, Blake says, is not, despite its material benefits, a fulfilment but a deprivation.

The first thing we have been deprived of, under this dispensation, is full consciousness. Blake images our condition as one of sleep; not the primordial slumber of the not yet awakened, but something else: "For Albion's sleep is not / Like Africa's, and his machines are woven with his life." Logic pursued exclusively, so Blake maintains, in the individual mind or the purposes of society, induces a state of somnambulism or nightmare. (There is a great deal of modern evidence to support this.) Albion has to wake up. Towards the end of the poem, this happens, and then the vision can proceed, and make clear to us what else we have been deprived of, restoring to us the things that were lost, until in the con-

clusion Albion stands once more in the full beauty and power of
living humanity before the face of God.

The Cartesian method and metaphor leads to a vision of man as a
disembodied mind, a spectre indeed. "Entering into the Reasoning
Power, forsaking Imagination, / They became Spectres." Man,
then, needs to be given back body and imagination, not in opposition to, but in completion of, his powers of thought. The united
power of body and imagination Blake calls "the Body of Divine
Analogy." He scarcely ever mentions the imagination, "the All
Glorious Imagination" as he calls it, without adding the phrase, "the
Divine Body." In his thought, body and imagination are inseparable,
and he identifies the two together with the Divine in the figure of
Jesus Christ, the Incarnate Word of God of the Christian religion.

After our disembodied powers of think have been restored to
full consciousness and reknit with body and imagination, there are,
in Blake's vision, two more stages of restitution before the work is
complete. These last two come at the very end of the poem. Albion
has awakened and arisen, the Redeemer has appeared in power and
majesty, and all things are restored—this is Judgement Day. Then
when the Spectre has at last been annihilated, we see this:

> . . . . . . at the clangor of the Arrows of Intellect
> The innumerable chariots of the Almighty appeared in Heaven,
> And Bacon and Newton and Locke, and Milton and Shakspear
>   and Chaucer . . .

Science and poetry, the great English traditions of logical and of
metaphoric thought embodied in their most noble representatives,
are restored each to each, to partake mutually in the final glory.
What is more, Blake tells us of their common activity in that state;
for they converse, he says, "in visionary forms dramatic," and in
a language whose "every Word and every Character was Human."
Language is given back to the mind, but we shall miss the import
of that last image unless we take it seriously. When Blake says that
every word is human it sounds like a truism; of course words are
human. This is not what he means. He is saying that every word
is at once a word and a human body and mind. Try it again as a

metaphor; it becomes much harder to manage and much more interesting. It is all part of Blake's consistently anthropomorphic thinking, "for Cities / are Men, fathers of multitudes, and Rivers and Mountains / Are also Men; everything is Human, mighty! sublime!" as he says in Chapter 2 of *Jerusalem*. With this as the crowning touch of his form of thought, Blake ends his vision, which is also his *Discours de la Méthode*.

The vision is extraordinary, but it is all the more important for not being exceptional. Each of Blake's insights—his diagnosis of our basic trouble as isolated emphasis on pure mental relations, our hypnotized acquiescence in the machine or nightmare, the absence of the human image—and his restoratives—imagination, the body, the reuniting of science and poetry, the turning to language, the anthropomorphic vision—these are confirmed and developed by poets innumerable, in the continuity and solidarity of the great poetic tradition of the West. To take a single example for the moment, the more valuable since it is in Cartesian terms, we might look at Coleridge's *Biographia Literaria*. Coleridge takes hold, in Chapters XII and XIII of that work, of the relation of Man to Method, of the *Sum*, man's irreducible affirmation of his being, and in a long footnote he criticizes Descartes' correlative *Cogito* which becomes abstraction and engine, on grounds partly philosophical and partly theological. In the opening sentence of Chapter XIII Descartes enters again, this time in company with Archimedes as if to epitomize the central condition and dilemma of scientific method in the present day, and later in this Chapter we come to the famous definition of the Imagination: "the living Power and prime Agent of all human perception, and a repetition in the finite mind of the eternal act of creation in the infinite I AM." There is a *Sum* in Coleridge's statement as there was in Descartes', but where for the latter, "I am" was a think, impersonal, mathematical and technological, for Coleridge the method which, no less than in Descartes, is the other term of Man's equation is a total, active, living, perceiving human organism, with, as part of its totality, the image of God implied by Coleridge's use of the I AM which is one of the names of the Divinity.

There is a suggestion here of a different metaphor for Man,

which is also a different Method, some concept of human thought which is to be integral, calling into play every power and faculty of mind and body. Something of what this method may be we are going to try to find out in the rest of this book. I am calling it, since Method is metaphor and also man, the Human Metaphor. The title is not my invention. Two poets have it. The first is Novalis, at the end of the eighteenth century, who jotted down in his notebook the phrase, "Man—metaphor." The other is Dylan Thomas, who died only a few years ago, and died young as Novalis did. The words, "Man be my metaphor" conclude one of his poems. Did he know Novalis? He may have, but whether or no, it is good to be reminded once again of the poetic tradition or dynasty, and of its steady and passionate preoccupation with this very matter, of Method and its intimate relation with the figure of Man.

So far, we have looked at the results, upon our image of ourselves, of the prevailing method, the Cartesian-scientific. We have seen how its apparent suppression of metaphor has merely resulted in the overt metaphor becoming crypto-metaphor in all of us, and producing in us a sense of loss or of a gap since this method with which we are now fused dismisses whatever lies between pure abstractions and the constructs, mental or mechanical, of those abstractions. This loss or gap concerns the natural world, the metaphoric properties of language, the imagination, and the body of man and society. We are ready now to consider the possibility of Method which would include and not exclude these added conditions. We have gained glimpses of such a possibility from the poets. We must not, however, for this reason fall back on the old way of thinking, that science has one method, poetry or art or humanities a totally different one. That was the belief behind the seventeenth-century rejection of metaphor as one of the instruments of science. The belief that scientific method is not metaphoric in action, that poetry is, and that science and poetry are quite separate is, as we have glimpsed in this Chapter and hope to see more clearly in the next, an illusion. All Method is figure, of universe and of Man. Yet this illusion has come to be accepted almost as dogma, and is to this day. This is serious, because what you believe determines what you will observe. Dogmatic belief in an illusion paralyzes the capacity to perceive evidence, no matter how plain or copious, which does not correspond with the beliefs held. It is not that the believer wilfully will not look; it is that he cannot see.

Only such a belief and paralysis could, it seems to me, have so obscured from us the great development over the last two or three hundred years of a discipline of intensive inquiry into Method, carried on by both poets and scientists (and of course the other dynasties as well, but we cannot manage them all here), admitting metaphor as part of its working, and an essential part. If we can shift our ground, remembering the point at which we began and the great communal work of being human, being man, built up by all of us and shared out among all the seven dynasties of ours, we shall be ready to go on: to consider metaphor and its relation to Method, taking counsel from poets and scientists, and then to catch sight of what I am going to call the battle of the metaphors in human Method, of long duration but coming apparently to a climax in our own time, a battle not at all between pro-metaphor poets and anti-metaphor scientists but fought out among the scientists themselves as to which metaphor to choose to work with in their researches into nature, a metaphor or method with sufficient energy within it to correspond with the native energy of the cosmos, working and dynamic, as it now appears to us.

Two

METAPHORS AND ENERGY

I

BEFORE WE GO ANY FURTHER, IT WILL BE AS WELL TO STOP and consider this notion of "metaphor," with which we have been making rather free. Is it not after all a restricted manoeuvre, involving two images, and concerning on the whole the professional poet; or, at most, a property of language?

In one sense, yes. Metaphor, as no doubt we were all taught at school, is a "figure of speech." It is inherent in language, rooting at the base of an infinite number of single words or phrases ("Is not your very Attention a Stretching-To?" as Carlyle asks) and closely related to the other main figures of speech and fiction and imagination, such as simile, personification, myth, and the extended narrative metaphor we call allegory. These are, we tend to suppose, the business of the poet. Yet all we have done so far is to name instances of metaphoric activity, not to characterize that activity itself. What is going on in metaphor itself?

Metaphor in its simplest form consists in the perception and exhibition of a relationship of correspondence between two separate and diverse entities or phenomena. In metaphor the mind sees and expresses an analogy, sometimes apparently material as when attention is drawn to physical resemblance—X is like Y, the simile—but always also, and sometimes exclusively, formal, as when Series X or Complex X or Happening X is seen to correspond with Series, Complex, or Happening Y in a set of one-to-one or more intricate relations. Within this binary system there is an inherent movement, towards fusion of the two terms: X becomes Y; indeed, in the classic form of poetic metaphor, X *is* Y. Man is a reed.

Looked at in this way, metaphor can be seen to accompany language, but it is not solely a property of words. Thought which uses words does not work this way because language works this way; language is like this because thought is. Words, and poetry above all, are the mind's attempt to shape an instrument for itself which shall be adequate to this essential method of the mind, but the method goes far beyond the vehicle of words. It seems possible that mathematics in its turn is just such a superb if exsanguine mythology; Suzanne Langer's work on music suggests that something of this sort of figuring goes on there, and it may well be a basic form of operation of all human thought, and an instrument of all seven dynasties. The poets themselves insist that it is not tied to words. It has its root in the establishing by the mind of connective relations, hitherto unexpressed if the thought is original and often only partly consciously perceived, between two mental events in order to understand better either or both of the two terms, or something else again for which the metaphor may be an interpretative instrument. I find I am paraphrasing Shelley here, and we may as well have a sentence or two direct from *A Defence of Poetry*, written in 1821. Speaking of "poets in the most universal sense of the word," he says, "Their language is vitally metaphorical; that is, it marks the before unapprehended relations of things and perpetuates their apprehension . . . These similitudes or relations are finely said by Lord Bacon to be 'the same footsteps of nature impressed upon the various subjects of the world'; and he considers them as the storehouse of axioms common to all knowledge."

The poet's concern with metaphor springs from his active use of this type of thinking. Figuring, in poetry, is never a matter of the mere technics of versifying, but a way into a method. Aristotle declares that this faculty for analogical invention and thought is the hallmark of the poet. In our period, however, because of our impoverished view of method and our separating of poetry and science, this needs further comment. It received it from Carlyle. In his essay on Goethe of 1828, included in *Critical and Miscellaneous Essays,* he calls this exercise of thought "the grand problem of the Poet." Then, however, he adds, "We do not mean mere metaphor and rhetorical trope: These are but the exterior concern, often but the scaffolding of the edifice which is to be built up (within our thoughts) by means of them . . . We speak of that Poetry which Masters write, which aims not at 'furnishing a languid mind with fantastic shows and indolent emotions,' but at incorporating the everlasting Reason of man in forms visible to his Sense and suitable to it; and of this we say that to know it is no slight task; but rather that, being the essence of all science, it requires the purest of all study for knowing it."

Poets refuse to relinquish their connection with science, and it is noticeable that it is the poets who have been for the last hundred and fifty years the most assiduous workers on method. They not only employ it, they write about it, giving us manuals on method as it were, and claiming that the method is relevant to science as well as to their own discipline. Shelley's *Defence of Poetry* is just such a manual of method, and we receive others, adapted to their widely differing personalities, from Coleridge, Carlyle, Mallarmé and Ezra Pound. The very variety of the commentators indicates the coherence and tenacity of the poetic tradition at this point. Coleridge, poet who was also philosopher, vast amorphous talker and thinker of genius, drug addict and painfully unhappy human being; Carlyle, rebarbative, awkward, sarcastic Scot who saw himself as "a wild Seer, shaggy, unkempt . . . an untutored energy, a silent, as it were unconscious strength"; Mallarmé moving with his debonair elegance and exquisite courtesy through the literary circles of Paris fifty years later; and, fifty years later again, the tormented political dynamiter, Ezra Pound the American—they all instruct us on method. We are going to look now at what the four poets above have to tell us, reserving comment on their methodology until later. At present what I want to adduce is the evidence. We will take them in chronological order.

First comes that section of *The Friend* (1809-10), headed "On the Grounds of Morals and Religion, and the Discipline of the Mind Requisite for a True Understanding of the Same," in which Coleridge considers, in Essays IV, VII and IX, "Method," "The Necessity of Ideas to Scientific Method," and "The Baconian Method Essentially One with the Platonic."

Coleridge presents method, first, as a matter of relations in the mind, enlivened, as he says, by thought and imagination. He then goes on to say that method is "employed in the formation of the understanding, and in the constructions of science and literature." He sees, as did Carlyle, the method as common to both great disciplines. What is more, he puts his finger on something we have already suggested, namely, that method constructs the mind at the same time as it constructs the constructions of that mind. He now goes on to consider the working principles of method. He sees two of them, the Principle of Preconception and the Principle of Progressive Transition.

In the first, Coleridge postulates that a previous act and conception of the mind is indispensable to directed thought or method. This primordial act of the mind, not wholly conscious, which asserts by prefiguring that which it is directed towards discovering, he calls by a number of names: a staple or starting-post in the mind; a leading thought; the initiative; a prior purpose; a precogitation. It is essentially antecedent to formulated thinking, and directs it in its research and its selection of evidence. Without this, no naturalist, Coleridge maintains, will ever receive "an auspicious answer from the oracle of nature." (We may note the metaphor as we go by.)

The second principle, that of Progressive Transition, declares that true method can never be merely a way of ordering or collecting in the mind, nor a mechanical received fashion of operating. Method, to justify itself, must generate within itself as part of its specific working a characteristic energy and movement forwards. As part of its essential and regular operation it tells the mind where to go and what to do next. It has a momentum towards future thought.

To this outline of a sketch for an energetics of speculative enquiry, Coleridge adds a further touch. The mind prefiguring and progressing in this way will come at length to the stage of formulation: hypothesis, theory, or statement of law. Yet Coleridge adds that this formulation will promote true method only "where the hypothesis is an exponential image or picture-language of an idea which is contained in it more or less clearly; or the symbol of an undiscovered law." Coleridge is, of course, thinking back to Bacon here, just as Shelley was in the passage I quoted earlier from the *Defence;* many of the poet-workers on method go back to Bacon, that ambivalent founder of so-called modern scientific method. Coleridge in the above passage, however, is saying, if I understand him aright, that a hypothesis is a figure (the iteration of image, picture and symbol in his sentence is telling and extraordinary) of what the prefiguring and progressive energy is directed towards; one term in a metaphor in which the object of research is the other. That the form of enquiry relates to what is being enquired into, every poet knows; but so, I believe, does any researcher who is aware of himself at this level of proceedings. At any rate, Coleridge in this remarkable hint sets side by side hypothesis, image and idea, and comes close to fusing them.

If some concept of energy in the mind is central to Coleridge's thought on method, it is no less so to Carlyle's. In his essay, "Signs of the Times" of 1829, he differentiates between two methods in the mind. The first he calls Mechanical, which provides a limited field of operation and interpretation but no more. (Coleridge also postulated a mechanical method, in his essay on *The Necessity of Ideas to Scientific Method,* and ascribed this to the sophists as against the opposing method of Plato.) The second is the Dynamic method. Those who operate by this, amongst whom Carlyle includes the poets, "without neglecting the Mechanical province, deal chiefly with the Dynamical; applying themselves chiefly to regulate, increase, and purify the inward primary powers of man . . . the instinctive, unbounded force, which Nature herself lent him, and still continues to him." We may notice in the same essay that for Carlyle an idea, and not simply the constructions of poets, may partake of this dynamic force. He cites the French Revolution as a case in point. For this man, too, ideas and poetry operate in unison, as do the respective functions of the mind, in terms of this central energy which moves them all. In *Heroes and Hero-Worship* of 1841 we find him saying, "We talk of faculties as if they were distinct, things separable; as if a man had intellect, imagination, fancy, etc. . . . We ought to know withal, and to keep forever in mind, that these divisions are at bottom but *names;* that man's spiritual nature, the vital Force which dwells in him, is essentially one and indivisible; that what we call imagination, fancy, understanding, and so forth, are but different figures of the same Power of Insight, all indissolubly connected with each other, physiognomically related."

It is the vital Force in man which Carlyle examines in his principal methodology, *Sartor Resartus,* where the force takes the form of metaphor and where he himself employs metaphor, as method, throughout, under the figure of his half-mad German Professor who is inventing a colossal Philosophy of Clothes. Carlyle sees in this force the constructive principle which shapes bodies first and then, to graze past Shakespeare for a moment, bodies forth language and metaphor itself. "Must not the Imagination weave Garments, visible Bodies, wherein the else invisible creations and inspirations of our Reason are, like Spirits, revealed, and first become all-powerful . . . ?" He identifies the body with this constructive process, and adds shortly after, "Language is the Flesh-Garment, the Body, of Thought. I said that Imagination wove this Flesh-Garment; and does not she? Metaphors are her stuff: examine Language; what, if you except some few primitive elements (of natural sound), what is it all but Metaphors, recognised as such, or no longer recognised . . . ? If those same primitive elements are the osseous fixtures in the Flesh-Garment, Language,—then are Metaphors its muscles and tissues and living integuments. An unmetaphorical style you shall in vain seek for." At the end of this passage he adds, with a reassuring touch of self-mockery, "Than which paragraph on Metaphors did the reader ever chance to see a more surprisingly metaphorical?"

If we end with metaphor in Carlyle, we begin with it in Mallarmé. Paradoxically enough for a poet reputed so obscure, it is he who comes up with the best definition of metaphor that I know. He deals with it as a process, and gives, as it were, a recipe for it: "To institute an exact relationship between the images, and that there detach itself from them a third aspect, fusible and clear, presented to divination." (I translate literally.)

We start with a relationship of images and the invocation of precision. (I hope we may take for granted that poetry is one of the most precise disciplines imaginable? Goethe says that it may be difficult for a mind accustomed to the exact sciences to realize that there is in poetry a precision of the imagination no less intensive, without which poetry would be simply impossible. We see it in various forms—a love of exact forms for their own sake, in Valéry's pursuit of mathematics and adoption of Leonardo da Vinci's device, *Ostinato rigore*, as his own; minute powers of observation passionately pursued, as in the Gerard Manley Hopkins Notebooks; the scrupulosity of any poet in the choice, use and placing of words.)

If exact relation between images is at the heart of metaphor and of poetry, this is not all. Out of the exactness must appear some *tertium quid*, which Mallarmé calls, a little guardedly, a fusible and clear third aspect. The precise relation, once established, has to prove itself fertile in the mind. Good metaphor has not merely exactitude but potential of development. The poet appeals (as do the scientists Cuvier and Lamarck, respectively) from precision as an isolated aim to a kind of fertile dynamic in the method. This "third aspect" gives metaphor, regarded in this way, an odd look of Hegel's dialectic; and indeed nineteenth-century German philosophy may well be driven by energy systems in abstract figures, as Edmund Wilson suggests in *To The Finland Station*, where he speaks of "the abstractions of the Germans" as "foggy and amorphous myths, . . . descending into reality in the role of intervening gods."

Mallarmé ends by telling us the purpose to which this dynamic is directed. It is, he says, presented to divination: groping, guesswork,—the French word for "to guess" is "deviner"—as in waterdivining, the half-conscious progress towards what is yet real and human knowledge. This is for Mallarmé part of the function of the poet, precision as in his sonnet, *Tombeau d'Edgar Poë*, "Donner un sens plus pur aux mots de la tribu"—to give a purer sense to the words of the tribe; and a larger aim which he calls "the orphic explanation of the world, which is the poet's one duty," attempted, he adds, by anyone who has ever written anything, genius or non-genius, consciously or unconsciously, since writing began.

Our last methodologist, whose thought shows a frame not unlike this, is Ezra Pound. He has written a number of rather polemical statements which come close to method, but I want to draw his contribution here from part of his great poem, the Cantos.

In Cantos LI to LXXXIV Pound turns our attention to China and its history. This for him is nothing new. He had previously published beautiful translations of Chinese poetry; now he is writing about Chinese history in this long work in which he tries to affirm the living past as he sees it and to flay out the dead matter, again as he sees it, from our present historical condition. In these Cantos, however, he not only introduces Chinese subject matter, he begins introducing Chinese ideograms. Some of them are names of historical characters, a few are those for objects or abstracts; but the often repeated ones have all to do with method and you have got to pay attention to them as such if you are to follow his thought and his poem. They cannot be passed over, as one tends to do with individual quotations in a language with which one is totally unfamiliar. These have, in an exact sense, to be reckoned with. They are built right in to what is going on.

From hearing my friends and students talk of reading Pound, and from my own experience at this point, I think many of the poet's readers are outraged at this. How can we be expected to wrestle with Chinese ideograms? Admittedly we had already probably read Pound's translations from the Chinese, together with those of Helen Waddell and Arthur Waley, as part of our general culture. But certainly for me, and I daresay for many of us in England and America, this was the spot where something of the real nature of Chinese language and thought, or say Chinese figuring, first confronted us as a direct challenge. On condition that we accept this, however imperfectly, we can hear what he has to say about method. His own exhibition of it is imperfect: Pound is not a sinologist and is sometimes in error in this extremely complex field. Yet it is an expert, Hugh Porteous, writing on "Ezra Pound and his Chinese Character" in a collection of essays by various hands, *An Examination of Ezra Pound,* published by New Directions in 1950, who says of Pound's amateur insight into Chinese characters, "Was it not Aristotle who announced that a man's genius was commensurate with his power to make good metaphors? Certainly one of the non-transferable endowments of genius appears to be the gift for analogical as against logical thinking . . . In this respect Pound exhibits all the signs of the greatest genius." (One may compare a remark in Hugh Kenner's *The Poetry of Ezra Pound,* "Ideogram, at least as a poetic principle, is not a Sinophile fad. It inheres in Aristotle on metaphor." And, later in the same book, "The Chinese ideograph, like the metaphor, deals in exceedingly condensed juxtapositions." The whole work is very valuable.)

In the table that follows are listed the principal ideograms, methodological in character, which Pound uses in the Cantos. Their names and the explanations of them come from the indispensable *Annotated Index to the Cantos of Ezra Pound* by J. H. Edwards and W. W. Vasse.[1] Then follows the context in the Cantos in which the ideogram makes its appearance. (Since it seemed simplest to tabulate this material, I have not kept the typographical arrangement of the poetry.) It would be a great advantage if at this point the reader could have beside him a copy either of the Cantos or of the Annotated Index, so as to be able to identify and contemplate these beautiful and stimulating little ideograms or picture-words at the same time as reading about them.

Character	Annotated Index	The Cantos[2]
1. chêng⁴ ming²	to regulate with the name: to define the correct terms; to rectify the names or terms: a true definition.	LX. He ordered 'em to prepare a total anatomy, et qu'ils veillèrent à la pureté du langage, et qu'on n'employât que des termes pro-

[1] University of California Press, 1957. See Appendix B, pp. 269 ff. The little numbers attached to the names of the ideograms refer not to footnotes in this text but occur in the original and are technicalities of Chinese lexicography.

[2] From *The Cantos of Ezra Pound,* Copyright 1934, 1948 by Ezra Pound. Reprinted by permission of New Directions, Publishers.

pres (namely CH'ing ming) LXVI. what is said there is rather a character than a true (ching ming) definition. It is a just observation.
LXVIII. to show U.S. the importance of an early attention to language for ascertaining the language. Ching Ming.

2. chêng, as above, alone — upright, true, exact, straight: clear as to definitions. — LXIII. exposition of technical terms.
LXVII. clear as to definitions CHING.

3. ming, as above, alone — bright, clear, intelligent; to understand, to cleanse, to illustrate: these are distinctions; Confucius, 20: the sun and moon, the total light process, the radiation, reception and reflection of light; hence the intelligence. Bright, brightness, shining. — LXXIV. in the light of light is the virtù.
LXXXIV. These are distinctions in clarity, ming, —these are distinctions.

4. hsin¹ jih⁴ — new + daily + new: to renovate, to make new daily: Day by day make it new; Confucius, 36: as the sun makes it new / day by day make it new / Yet make it new again. — LIII. MAKE IT NEW . . . Day by day make it new. LIV. (Ideograms repeated.)

5. pien⁴ — to transform, to change: a word to make change. — LVII. seeking the transmutation of metals/ seeking a word to make change.

6. chung¹ — the middle; the axis, centre, pivot: I am for balance; Confucius, 103: an axis round which something turns. — LXX. I am for balance. LXXVI. the word is made perfect/ better gift can no man make to a nation (also includes ch'êng ideogram; see 7 below.)

			LXXVII. Chung/ in the middle.
			LXXXIV. There is our norm of spirit/ our (ideogram) whereto we pay our homage.
7. ch'êng	honesty, sincerity: the word is made perfect; Confucius, 20: the precise definition of the word, pictorially the sun's lance coming to rest on the precise spot verbally.		See item 2 under 6 above.
8. ch'êng²	to complete: bringest to focus.		LXXVIII. chêng bringest to focus/ chêng.
9. hsien¹ hou⁴	before + after: first and last, successive: what precedes and what follows.		LXXVII. To know what precedes and what follows will assist your comprehension of process.
10. chih⁴	will, purpose: *directio voluntatis* as lord over the heart; Confucius, 22: the will, the direction of the will.		LXXVII. their aims as one/ directio voluntatis as lord over the heart.
11. tao⁴	a path, the truth, the doctrine, the way; Confucius, 22: the process, an orderly movement under lead of the intelligence.		LXXVIII. a system measured and gauged to human requirements/ inside the nation or system/ and cancelled in proportion/ with what is used and worn out.
12. tz'u² ta² (latter used wrongly)	speech, words: an expression or phrase, message + intelligent, successful; to succeed: to succeed in saying exactly what you wish to say; what matters is to get it across . . . In language it is simply required that it convey the meaning.		LXXIX. in discourse what matters is to get it across/ e poi basta.

13. jên² perfect virtue, human-heartedness: *humanitas*; Confucius, 22: humanity, in the full sense of the word, "manhood." The man and his full contents. LXXXII. and had more humanitas.

14. wu⁴ chu⁴ chang³ do not + assist + to grow: don't work so hard . . . let it grow naturally; variation of Mencius, II, I, ii, 16: "Let not the mind forget its work, but let there be no assisting the growth of that nature." LXXXIII. "Non combaattere" said Giovanna/ meaning, as before stated, don't work so hard.

15. fu² chieh² agree + token, credential: a warrant, commission. (*Halves of a tally stick* is translation of only the fu²). LXXVII. can they again put one together/ as the two halves of a seal, or a tally stick?

As we read these, even in isolation as I have presented them here, there is audible the same note we have met before: the devotion to precision, to the purification of the language, to equilibrium which holds in the midst of change and growth and process, and is in its turn ordered and directed by the will and the mind. All this could have been said in words, our Western kind of words, I mean. Pound, however, adds the ideograms at this very point, as if to compel us to look at figuring in the form of image, not just at concept or principle. The figure is not a picture or illustration; it is part of the process which is going on, the operation of the poetic mind, where image, idea and language do their work together.

The final image given above was that of the two halves of a tally stick. Pound uses this, the figure of that very process in the mind we call metaphor or analogy, the exact correspondence between two patterned objects, more than once in Canto LXXVII, from which the examples quoted are drawn. He has not yet finished with it, however. In Canto LXXXII he harks back to this central image, although he does not this time repeat the ideogram which is why I did not include it with the other examples in the table. He is writing in this Canto a very beautiful hymn to the earth; and in the midst of it he puts in the final stage of this metaphor of his. "Man, earth: two halves of the tally."

I am going to try now to put together and sum up what our four poets have suggested to us about method. Method resides in a central force or energy in the body-mind, to be construed as dynamic rather than mechanical, which operates in figures. This organic energy prefigures what it is enquiring into, and generates its own directed forward momentum by cooperation with its figures. These consist of precise relations between images which are also ideas, which relations must give rise to further figures by which the mind may grope its way forward on its due progress of divination. Language, which is to be constantly purified and searched in accordance with these purposes, accompanies and assists the organism in its operation, but does not delimit the figuring process. The aim of the activity is to arrive at temporary formulations, whether scientific or poetic, which shall assist in the interpretation of the world and the mind, in terms of one another, and which shall once again further the advance of method itself.

So say the poets. Does this method of theirs agree at all with what scientists are doing, or do the latter regard themselves as off on a different track altogether?

II

There is, of course, much of science, and indeed of any discipline of the mind including poetry, which does not work in this way. We all know the indispensable bread-and-butter ways which come nearer to plain logic or sheer plodding, and only a dilettante would reject or look down on them. We are not claiming any exclusive rights for the type of method which the poets are enquiring into. The fact remains, however, that when science becomes speculative in any sense, asking questions which entail not just the getting of information but its interpretative shaping, then something very like the method expounded by the poets does seem, in fact, to take over.

Heuristics, that study of the ways in which discoveries, solutions to problems and original advances in thought and knowledge are made, is relatively new. It seems to me to get its first clear formulation in the work of Henri Poincaré, the mathematician, published in 1904, *Science et Méthode,* in which he discusses the figuring and non-logical methods of the mathematical imagination in all its originality. Once started—that is to say, once we had decided to look at the evidence from this point of view—heuristics has almost a superabundance of historical and contemporary evidence to work with. It is clear that many a scientific genius, when his proceedings are examined, seems to have worked in much the way that the poets have been describing.

The best survey of this kind of thought among the great scientists is to be found in Arthur Koestler's book *The Sleep-Walkers,* 1959. He writes about Copernicus, Kepler, Galileo and Newton. (Newton, as any biography of his shows, is a classic or notorious case of a mind making vast intuitive-imaginative leaps forward. The gaps in between were capable of being filled in with the normal steps of logical progression, and Newton often filled them in himself in this way; but the advance was not made by means of such steps.) Arthur Koestler sets out to show precisely this: that scientific thought of real importance does not proceed according to sensible methods, of induction or deduction or any other recognized procedure. In this manifestation of itself it is neither rational nor altogether conscious. The writer's choice of metaphor, that of somnambulism, serves him well, since the sleepwalker is active and often highly controlled and dextrous yet is certainly not in a condition which we could call waking consciousness. It is interesting that Goethe applies this same metaphor to Shakespeare and the operations of his genius; applies it almost in irritation, one feels in the context, at the apparent combination of total mastery and total unself-consciousness in that most enigmatic genius of them all.

Many contemporary scientists—I think of Max Planck, for example, or Fred Hoyle—describe their own mental operations in these terms: "seizing upon some happy idea," "guessing by a kind of inspiration a set of figures." It is one of Michael Polanyi's great services to thought and method that this problem, as it occurs in science, has had his constant attention, from *The Logic of Liberty,*

1951, where he talks already of the need for a good guess at the beginning of scientific research, and of half-consciously perceived clues which must direct it; through *Personal Knowledge* where the tacit component of all conscious thought is postulated, and a relation set up through this and the conscious mind between the constructs of the mind and the phenomena of the world: "The constructions of mathematics will tend, therefore, to disclose those hidden principles of the experienced world of which some scattered traces had first stimulated the imaginative process by which these constructions were conceived" (in that last sentence, the word "imaginative" in the original version of the manuscript was written as "poetic"; perhaps we should have Variorum editions of the works of scientists as well as of those of the poets?) His most recent and developed examination of this principle is in a paper, "The Unaccountable Element in Science," published in *Philosophy,* Vol. XXXVII, No. 139, January 1962.

Michael Polanyi considers intuition in science as continuous with perception, a highly developed and valuable skill which cannot be formulated in solely intellectual terms and which is essential to all progress and discovery in science. Method, as here outlined, closely resembles that method which the poets have been feeling after: Coleridge's prefiguring and inarticulate sense of direction, Carlyle's inclusion of the body in the figuring process. The likeness holds good, too, with that divining which Mallarmé postulates at the heart of metaphor. This kind of divination is inherent in the whole course of research pursued by the skilled individual, but Michael Polanyi maintains that it operates also after the point of formulation of the hypothesis or theory. How to tell a "good" theory from an unsatisfactory one? This too appears to be a matter of divination: "But at the stage when we have to make up our minds about the merits of a discovery its future repercussions are unknown . . . The mark of true discovery is not its fruitfulness but the intimation of its fruitfulness" (*Personal Knowledge*). The intimation of fruitfulness—we called it fertility in speaking of metaphor in Mallarmé's characterization; the metaphor is the same. At this point also enters Carlyle's concept of energy. It appears to be typical of the good scientific theory as well as of the good meta-

phor that from its very fittingness and precision should emanate
in the mind a divining impetus which communicates, to the organism receiving it, hints, unformulable yet convincing, of future interpretative power. What is interesting is that the communication
is frequently accompanied by a great access of energy within that
same organism. There are recorded cases of this—of an Archimedes
lifted out of his bath to course down the street in a naked, shouting,
lonely triumph, of a Kepler flung for an hour or two into fiery dithy-
rambs of poetry. It seems that what produces this, and even the
smaller exaltations of 'having an idea' in more ordinary minds, is
not a sense of "something accomplished, something done," nor
even a sense of something explained; rather it is the intimation of
potential, a sense of power and discovery still to come, dimly yet
passionately perceived.

This energy, communicated to the mind-body organism by the
latter's sense of nascent divinatory power in its own figuring, is
the characteristic of a good metaphor, hypothesis or theory, idea.

The word "good" is, I realize, rather tendentious. Poets and
critics do speak of good metaphors, however, just as scientists
speak, in the same sense, of good questions or even of good errors.
"Good" refers here to those figures which have the fertile energy
we have been thinking about; yet we do perhaps need to remind
ourselves, since we are using the figure of energy, that energy is
not confined to good ideas or good minds, in a wider sense. False
ideas, and figurings, in political demagoguery or the excesses of
revivalistic religion for instance, can for a time at least produce
great energy, though possibly more in the practical than in the speculative field. In our age we know that to our cost. Yet the evidence
does seem to show that energy of this diverted or perverted type
is a manifestation not ultimately of fertility and fulfilment but of
frustration; that falsehood, evil and madness are not, thank God,
a *perpetuum mobile*. Aberrant forms of energy do not prove to be
what the sixteenth-century English poet so surprisingly says that
true love is, "a durable fire / In the *mind* ever burning"—the emphasis is mine. Possibly only energy which is in some real way directed towards the interpretation of the world and human life
(though this may require an energy of destruction at times as well

as that of construction) is genuinely self-generating. Michael Polanyi, in *Personal Knowledge,* says that this fertility must mean
"fertility of truth": "You cannot define the indeterminate veridical
powers of truth in terms of fruitfulness, unless 'fruitfulness' is itself qualified in terms of the *definiendum.* When we say that Coper-
nicanism was fruitful, we mean that it was a fruitful source of
truth."

Self-generating energy in the mind accompanies those good figures which have genuine interpretative potential. If this energy is a
mark of truth, it may also be the means by which we recognize
beauty; possibly it *is* beauty. The young poet may have uttered
more than a pious commonplace or aspiration when he connected
them, supported as he is by so many scientists.

Aesthetics are not our business, but it is conceivable that perhaps a fertile and communicable energy which flows out of and into
method, in these terms, is one of the properties of a great work of
art. Such works appear to possess free available energy which they
impart to, or exchange with, the attending mind. I first became
aware of this while listening to a Beethoven piano sonata finely
played (the transmission of energy seems to me to work better in live
situations than in mechanically recorded ones, but this may be only
personal idiosyncrasy). The music heightened my own mental
vitality and sent it spinning, profitably, along its own characteristic paths, enlivened by the formal vigour of the music. So Carlyle says, of a book, that it had "in a high degree excited us to self-
activity, which is the best effect of any book." Perhaps the very
"aesthetic pleasure" we derive from such situations is a merely
secondary result of the primary event, a considerable access of
energy within our own organisms, that Energy of which Blake says,
in a wonderful figure in *The Marriage of Heaven and Hell,* that it
is eternal delight.

This concerns, once again, not merely art or poetry but science
too. The notions of beauty and of a fertile energy superadded on
to the foundations of exactitude are to be found in science, in the
scientific equivalent of the poetic metaphor which is, broadly, the
hypothesis or theory. Of this we find Michael Polanyi saying in
Personal Knowledge that the affirmation of a great scientific theory

is in part an expression of delight. He goes on to compare a scientific theory and a work of art explicitly, and adds a little later, "I believe that by now three things have been established beyond reasonable doubt: the power of intellectual beauty to reveal truth about nature; the vital importance of distinguishing this beauty from merely formal attractiveness; and the delicacy of the test between them, so difficult that it may baffle the most penetrating scientific minds . . . In this empirical guidance of our groping by the facts lies all the difference—elusive and yet utterly decisive—between a merely formal advance and a new insight into the nature of things" (p. 149).

We may remember now the poets' insistence, particularly Mallarmé's and Pound's, that method in metaphor is not only exactitude in the figure but potential of development in that figure. In other words, the "figure" in "figure of speech" is closer to the figure in a dance than to Euclid. An exact metaphor is not always endowed with this fertility. May I give an example from my own poetry?

I tried for years to find, as poets are always doing, a descriptive analogy for one of the splendours of America, the colours which the great wooded landscapes of that country in its eastern states take on in the autumn. Trees turn colour in the frosts of Europe too, but only in America have I seen the astonishing colours of wide maplewoods, whole hillsides blazing in a range that runs from dark blood-crimson through vermilion, flame, orange, gold, salmon pink, lemon yellow, off-white. I had tried a number of metaphors for it, mostly flame and sunset, and was dissatisfied. Two autumns ago, driving through this annual transfiguration, I suddenly hit on what seemed the right one: the leafage of these trees has precisely the colour range of the blossoms on the springtime azaleas. I was delighted with the exactitude, yet disappointed later, for the metaphor, though exact, will take me no further. I cannot think with it; merely note its exactness and leave it there. A certain amount of metaphor met with in poetry is of this kind. It gives its own pleasure, as Rilke does when he compares the sound of a peal of carillon bells, lingering momentarily in the sky and then vanishing, to a bunch of grapes hanging, with Silence eating them off, one

by one. It is fitting but not fertile. In greater poems, and in great
poets for the most part, it is harder to find metaphors of this partial
sort. All the figures work, have energy or lend the mind energy to
work and to work further. That is to say, according to our present
line of thought, they are beautiful, beauty being considered as just
such a dynamic heuristic, whether we meet it in the figures of science, those of poetry, or elsewhere. It is exactly such a forward-
moving or prophetic energy that the chosen metaphor, within the
method in use. has to supply.

With these thoughts in our minds, we will move on now and
look at what I called earlier the battle of the metaphors: identifying
the main metaphors that have been employed, for nature, since the
seventeenth century, discerning or divining if we can the inherent
energy in them, and observing the work of selection and prefer-
ment of them, on the part of the great minds who turn them to use.

III

There have been, since the beginning of the seventeenth century
and of specifically "modern" thought, six recurring metaphors for
nature. There may well be more than six, just as there are sure to
be further examples of these six which I am unfamiliar with. My
list is not exhaustive, but it represents metaphors which I have
come upon frequently in my own reading and can vouch for. The
six figures compare nature to a temple, a labyrinth, a gambler, a
laboratory, a language and a machine. (I omit the turn of thought
and speech, not uncommon among scientists, in which nature is
thought of as a woman, "Mother Nature" as it were; I think this is
only a remnant of mythological thought, not a working figure any
more.)

Two things may be noted. The first is the prevalence of metaphor in general. This need not seem surprising where language is
being used, since, as we have seen, language is essentially metaphoric; but it is perhaps surprising to find scientists so involved in
it. And that brings me to the second thing—that the metaphors are
used by scientists and poets alike, along with other types of think-

ers. A figure for something as basic as nature involves, apparently, a number of the dynasties of workers on man and method. It may conceivably involve them all.

To start with we shall look at the first four figures, see what we can gather from them, and then go on to the last two, which are by far the most widespread and important.

Nature as temple—users of this figure include Novalis, Erasmus Darwin, the poet-scientist and grandfather of Charles Darwin, and, in a very famous poem indeed, Baudelaire. Novalis, when he is thinking about research in the natural sciences, turns his thought into an allegory and uses for its setting the legendary temple at Sais in Egypt. The apprentices or neophytes, *Die Lehrlinge zu Sais* (1798) as the title has it, are gathered here to pursue their search, and the final aim of each one is to lift the veil from the statue of the goddess which the temple contains. A little note added by the author to the unfinished story says that in the end the one who lifted the veil saw to his amazement that the goddess's face was his own; in another version of the tale, Novalis says it was the face of the searcher's beloved. There is also a veiled figure of Nature at the heart of Erasmus Darwin's *Temple of Nature*. He gave that title to his second long scientific poem, published in 1803, in which he recounts a pilgrimage into and through the temple, undertaken by the hierophant who would penetrate the secrets of nature. (Look for the veiled figure of nature in Shelley too, in Act II, Scene IV, of *Prometheus Unbound,* 1820, where the great figure of Demogorgon in the cave sits veiled upon a shadowy throne.) Next enters Baudelaire, and his poem *Correspondances.* The first stanza has an extraordinary statement and elaboration of the metaphor we are considering:

> La Nature est un temple, où de vivants piliers
> Laissent parfois sortir de confuses paroles.
> L'homme y passe à travers des forêts de symboles,
> Qui l'observent avec des regards familiers.

> (Nature—a temple, where the pillars live
> And sometimes utter speech-like undertone.
> Man threads that forest of symbols, and they give
> Him speaking looks, both knowing and well-known.)

Here the very temple is alive and is half-fused with language, so that the poet's figure is overflowing into the fifth of our six metaphors, nature as language.

Nature as labyrinth—Francis Bacon speaks of nature as a labyrinth in the Preface to his Great Instauration in the early seventeenth century; and one of his works, on his own method, is called *Filum Labyrinthi*, the clue to the maze. Galileo uses this figure. So does Robert Hooke, one of the original scientist members of the Royal Society, and a great user of metaphors, as we shall see. Erasmus Darwin produces it also, along with the clue of thread which is the answer to the puzzle, in *The Temple of Nature.*

Nature as gambler—Goethe, in a conversation with Falk in 1809, speaks of nature as seated at a gaming table, crying *"Au double!"* as Goethe says, and restaking the winnings every time. It is interesting to find this metaphor turning up in a recent work on biology by Gaylord Simpson, Colin Pittendrigh, and L. H. Tiffany, *Life: An Introduction to Biology*, 1957, where evolution is spoken of as a lottery, in which there are tickets with no future, those with a limited future, and winning tickets.

Nature as a workshop or laboratory—the first example of this that I know[3] is in the work of Herder, the German philosopher. Writing in 1784, he calls the globe a workshop for the production of new forms and a laboratory for experiment and research on them. Both metaphors recur, in the same kind of context, in Carlyle's *Sartor Resartus*, written in 1830-31; there the world is called "the terrestrial workshop," and the writer exclaims, "How thou fermentest and elaboratest, in thy great fermenting-vat and laboratory of an Atmosphere, of a World, O Nature!" That we all work at the world is said by Novalis in Part II, *Die Natur*, of *Die Lehrlinge zu Sais* and by Dylan Thomas again, "This world which is each man's work." That the world works at itself Renan is saying in 1863 in the *Vie de Jésus* and Nietzsche in the pre-1888 notes in *Der Wille zur Macht*,

[3] But Dr. Joseph Needham in *Science and Civilisation in China*, Cambridge University Press, Vol. II, p. 278, quotes a far earlier example, Robert Fludd, 1574-1637, who "pictures God as a chemist rather than a mathematician, with the world for his 'elaboratory' " in his *Medicina Catholica.*

only here the workshop has become a studio and the world is a self-producing work of art. In 1889 the image of nature as a workshop, complete with wood shavings, recurs in the poem which Alfred Russell Wallace, the inventor with Charles Darwin of the theory of natural selection, appends to his biological work, *Darwiniana*. In this poem nature is also compared to a painter's pallette (the work of art again, in process of creation), and to a poem, so that here too there is a link with the metaphor of nature as language.

Let us pause here for a moment and see what we have got so far, for out of these first four metaphors which seem so disparate a common ground is emerging.

Three of the figures seem to compare nature with a place—a temple, a labyrinth, a workshop or laboratory. Yet these are not just places, but places where something is going on. A temple, the first of the metaphors, is of course a sacred fane, but if we see it here merely as a place where people go to worship we shall miss the point, and certainly none of the poets use it in that way. They have, I daresay, a nobler and truer idea of what a temple, and worship, may be, for in this figure the temple is a place of intellectual striving, of discovery and effort, as indeed any true place of worship must be though we tend to forget this nowadays. Michael Polanyi speaks in *Personal Knowledge* of Christian worship as heuristic vision. The labyrinth, again, is a place, a maze—and it awaits and demands its challenger, the mind which shall find its way to the centre and then by its own thread of thought find its way out again. (Our commonplace metaphor, "I have lost the thread of what I was saying," implies that our everyday thought is some sort of labyrinth which we must find our way through, unravelling, and discovering, or losing ourselves temporarily, as we go.) Gambling, next, is a speculative activity directed towards the future and the unknown. The very word 'speculation' is entirely at home in the two worlds, of actual gambling whether in casino or stock exchange and of thinking, as if language facilitated our passage here from external to internal action. Poets and scientists use the image of gambling in connection with thought. Among the poets, you will find this metaphor in Paul Valéry and, supremely perhaps, in Stéphane Mallarmé. It forms the key image for his long poem, *Un Coup de Dés,* and he sums it up in the poem's last words: "Toute Pensée émet un Coup de Dés"—every thought casts forth a throw of the dice. Michael Polanyi uses the metaphor in connection with scientific research in *Personal Knowledge* ("Research is a gamble in which nothing is left to chance") and for the scientific vocation in *The Logic of Liberty,* "Scientists spend all their time betting their lives, bit by bit, on one personal belief after another." The metaphor of gambling is closely connected with the activity of guessing, that guesswork for which Poe puts in an impassioned plea, on behalf of both scientists and poets, in *Eureka* in 1848, and with "groping" as a method of nature and mind, as seen by Teilhard de Chardin and Michael Polanyi. And this brings us to the fourth metaphor, the laboratory, since that is precisely the place where such a questing activity is carried on. The figure of the workshop suggests a place where objects, whether of use or of art, are being made, and presumably, improved as time goes on; but the laboratory is the place of experiment and speculation and rigour and groping all at once, and, it seems to me, undoubtedly the place in our generation and culture where thought has a chance of being most alive.

All four metaphors, then, set up an analogy between nature and human activity; figuring one process by another process. Nature is compared not just to any activity, however, but the forward-directed and divining form of energy which we have been investigating with the poets' help. The energetics of figuring speculation within the human organism of body and mind are taken here as the exact and divinatory figure for the working universe, "this *active* universe," as Wordsworth calls it and the italics are his. In each of these four metaphors, method itself becomes the figure for nature. We see now that the four are in reality only one, and their, or its, tendency to coalesce with the figure of nature-as-language is not merely accidental, for that figure, too, is another aspect of this single metaphor, perhaps the most central of all five.

Nature as language is a very extensive metaphor, both in the number of instances of it and the number of forms it takes. It is ancient, but we shall be concerned with it only during the last three and a half centuries. To take some of the forms first, it may appear in the form of nature as alphabet, as with Bacon, Hooke, Linnaeus, Carlyle; nature as grammar and syntax, with Hooke,

Oken, Carlyle; nature as a secret language with Vico, Goethe, Schelling; nature as a cipher in Novalis and Emerson; nature as full
speech or a volume in Bacon, Galileo, Hooke, Coleridge, Carlyle,
Emerson. I should like to quote two of the most developed and or-
namented examples of this metaphor, one from the work of a scientist, one from that of a poet:

> A Collection of all varieties of Natural Bodies . . . where an
> Inquirer . . . might peruse, and turn over, and spell, and read the
> Book of Nature, and observe the Orthography, Etymologia, Syn-
> taxis, and Prosodia of Nature's Grammar, and by which as with
> a Dictionary, he might readily turn to and find the true Figures,
> Composition, Derivation, and Use of the Characters, Words,
> Phrases, and Sentences of Nature, written with indelible and
> most exact, and most expressive Letters, without which Books it
> will be very difficult to be thoroughly a Literatus in the Language
> and Sense of Nature.
>
> (Hooke, *Discourse of Earthquakes,* 1705)

> We speak of the Volume of Nature: and truly a Volume it is,
> whose Author and Writer is God. To read it! Dost thou, does man
> so much as well know the Alphabet thereof? With its Words,
> Sentences, and grand descriptive Pages, poetical and philosophi-
> cal, spread out through Solar Systems, and thousands of Years,
> we shall not try thee. It is a Volume written in celestial hiero-
> glyphs, in the true Sacred-writing; of which even Prophets are
> happy that they can read here a line and there a line. As for your
> Institutes and Academies of Science, they strive bravely; and
> from amid the thick-crowded, inextricably intertwisted hiero-
> glyphic writing, pick-out, by dextrous combination, some Letters
> in the vulgar Character, and therefrom put together this and the
> other economic Recipe, of high avail in Practice. That Nature is
> more than some boundless Volume of such Recipes, or huge
> well-nigh inexhaustible Domestic-Cookery-Book, of which the
> whole secret will in this manner one day evolve itself, the fewest
> dream.
>
> (Carlyle, *Sartor Resartus*)

The very range and variety of this metaphor tell us something
of its nature. For this is not simply speculation free and at large,
but speculation espousing the traditional forms of man's greatest

instruments for thought, those systems of figures which at once limit his thinking and give it its greatest power and scope. It is the same figure as the previous four, but made more definite.

At this point a very interesting, yet at first sight fantastic, question arises: what language is the book of nature written in? It is raised by Galileo, astronomer and working scientist, and that is proper, for we are coming to the battle of the metaphors, and it is the scientists who debate it, with only incidental interpolations by the poets. Galileo says, in his work entitled *Il Saggiatore:*

> Philosophy [sc. Science] is written in that most august book, which for ever stands open before our eyes (I mean the universe) but which we cannot understand if we do not first learn to understand the language, and familiarize ourselves with the characters, in which it is written. It is written in the language of mathematics, and the characters are triangles, circles, and other geometric figures, by means of which alone is it possible, humanly speaking, to understand a word of it. Without this, there can be nothing but a useless twisting and turning in a dark labyrinth.

Cast your eyes back to the quotation from Hooke, the first of the two longer passages cited above. The utterances of the two scientists make a beautiful pair, yet differ as to the language of nature's book. Galileo says it is a book of mathematics, specifically geometry. Hooke says it is a book written in words, sentences, and—you will notice from the insertion of the word "prosodia"—ultimately in poetry.

One might think that here we had found the point of battle in the metaphors; but all we have found is a point of difference, perfectly genuine but no ultimate cause of hostility at this stage.

Since speculative method, in the mind, is what we have been considering, I let poems and hypotheses run along parallel with each other in our enquiry, wanting to indicate their analogies—we are all too ready to underline their differences if we so much as ever put the two together. This does not mean, however, that metaphors or poems, ideas, and hypotheses in science are identical. They differ, obviously, in three important ways: in the obligatory tendency in scientific method and formulation of hypotheses towards quantity and mathematics; in verification; and in supersession—by which I mean the sequence by which a new scientific hypothesis can completely oust an older one.

The use of mathematical figures and the use of speech figures is a real difference. What the main points of difference and likeness are here will have to wait until such time as we know more about mathematics as a mythology and about poetry as a system of exact forms. Moving on to the next two differences, we all know that a scientific hypothesis is subject to experimental verification in terms of "facts" and mathematics whilst a poem is not subject to test in this way. Also, a new and better scientific hypothesis supersedes an older one, pushes it right out of the way and takes over, whereas no good poem since the beginning of speech has ever been superseded or ousted by another, nor ever will be. Yet to deny any verification to poems is to fall into the heresy which denies poetry any connection with reality or truth and relegates it to what in the seventeenth century was called, in this very context, "a dream of our imagination" and in the twentieth century was called emotive or non-referential speech, or pseudo-statement. Similarly to deny any progression in poetry, from earlier to later poets, is to impair the poets' own sense of their tradition. Poets operate, as do scientists, in a world of realities and time and change. It is not merely the poets, one may observe incidentally, who want to hold things together at this point, asserting unity rather than disunity with scientific and experimental disciplines. We might ponder the utterance of the English painter Constable, (quoted by E. H. Gombrich in *Art and Illusion*, 1960), "Painting is a science, and should be pursued as an enquiry into the laws of nature. Why, then, may not landscape painting be considered a branch of natural philosophy, of which pictures are but the experiments?" To this astonishing statement Dr. Gombrich adds this, "It is only in one respect that we should perhaps amend his formulation. What a painter inquires into is not the nature of the physical world but the nature of our reactions to it."

In science, certainly, attention and method are directed towards the interpretation of relations between phenomena, in isolation from the method and the mind (though certain areas of modern physics now offer an exception to this rule). A mind speculating in the poetic mode, however, draws into itself the very facts it is thinking about, so that it can not only think about them but think with them. For poetry, all objects and happenings in the universe are for thinking with, and phenomena or events are always available to poetry as method, at the same time as they are available as objects of contemplation. Poems are often verifiable, in human terms, in what they say, their inherent insight and wisdom concerning the human situation in general. Their more essential verification or justification, however, lies, I believe, in their continuing energy as instruments for divination, that is to say, as method. Great poems appear to be methodologically and heuristically inexhaustible. Never becoming totally detached from the parent method, they tend to merge back, as do phenomena they deal with, into the central energy of the method of figuring speculation itself, which appears to be common to the mind no matter what area it is working in, and which does not seem to change from age to age. They therefore remain varying exercises in a constant method. Scientific procedure, on the other hand, separates facts from method and method from mind. Isolated in this way from the parent energy of speculation itself, the constructions become liable to a different modality of change and perhaps to a different time-scale, for it seems to me that we need more and more to realize that there is no one over-all commanding time-scale, but a series of different ones, probably connected with, or at least manifested in, the different ways in which structures change.

These are differences, certainly. Yet the battle of the metaphors does not reside here, and Coleridge may have been right when he set image and idea and hypothesis side by side in the mind at the working point of formulation of hypotheses. The battle is the result of certain consequences of the experimental-mathematical or modern scientific way of thinking.

An interesting discussion of these consequences forms part of the theme of Dr. Joseph Needham's *Science and Civilisation in China,* Cambridge University Press. I quote from Vol. III, 1959, but there is much relevant matter in Vol. II, 1956, as well: "The Gali-

lean revolution did destroy the organic world-view which medieval
Europeans had possessed, to some extent in common with the Chinese, replacing it by a world-view essentially mechanistic. . . . But
the dramatic irony of fate brought it about that by the time of the
death of Newton himself (1727) the seed of a new organic view of
the world, destined ultimately to replace or correct the mechanistic
view, had been sown by Leibniz" (pp. 157-58). Here is the battle
of the metaphors; certain scientists (may we remind ourselves that
Leibniz here quoted is a very eminent mathematician indeed?) upholding nature as organism; certain other scientists upholding the
last of our six metaphors, nature as machine.

The figure of nature as machine is, I am told, an ancient one,
reaching back into medieval times;[4] but in our civilization it really
comes into its own with the "celestial mechanics" of Newton. Here
is the cosmos as machine, and the theologian Paley who in his
Natural Theology of 1802 likens the universe to a watch and de-
duces from it a hypothetical but absent God, the Celestial Watch-
maker. The metaphor runs steadily and increasingly through the
nineteenth century—"the Machine of the Universe—alas!" as Carlyle
exclaims in *Heroes and Hero-Worship* in 1841. It underlies the
whole deterministic outlook in science, is inherent in the Darwinian
theory, is very much with us today. It reaches over, as it must do,
into becoming also the metaphor for organisms and for humans.
Descartes speculated whether animals were not machines, and it is
only very recently, in modern studies of animal behaviour, that
this trend has been reversed. As for man, one may think immediately of La Mettrie and his *L'Homme Machine* of 1748; but before
this the English poet Rochester was talking of man, contemptuously,
as "the thinking Engine" in 1675, while Bacon himself, already
deeply interested in technology, makes the curious and typical attempt to turn his *Novum Organum,* belying the implications of his
title, into an automatic and mechanical method of would-be scientific thought. As for the ubiquity and respectability of the metaphor
today, open almost any scientific work and run your eye down the
page. It will not be long before you come upon the word "mecha-

---

[4] I owe this information to Dr. Siegfried Wenzel, of the University of
North Carolina.

nism," employed for structures and operations in biology, genetics, psychology, social science, neurology and those studies of the brain which are employing as models the mechanical constructs of the cybernetics industry, the "electronic brain" in fact, which crystallizes pretty exactly this very metaphor we are talking about. So accepted nowadays is the word "mechanism" that I believe those who use it fail to see that it is a metaphor, let alone its implications.

You can hear, probably, that I find it hard to be fair to this metaphor. Poets are very uneasy with it. Some of the uneasiness in Blake we saw already in Chapter I. One of the clearest commentators on it is Carlyle. By 1829, when he published his essay "Signs of the Times," he was noting with dismay its advance and how it seemed to be moving from supremacy in the realm of inanimate and animate nature towards an equal supremacy over the mind: "Not the external and physical alone is now managed by machinery, but the internal and spiritual also"; he mentions particularly the spheres of religion, psychology and politics.

A poet or two protesting may not seem very significant; but remember that remark of Dr. Needham's quoted earlier, that a countertrend to this, an organic image of nature, was growing up at the same time and is destined, so he says, to replace or at least rectify the mechanistic one. If the poets protest, the scientists do too. The examples of our first five metaphors are perhaps modest evidence of this other trend, but there are in existence clearer notes than these, which we should also hear. We will start with recent instances, and move backwards.

It is to me a curious thing that the two modern instances, of which I am aware, of this contemporary rejection of the machine metaphor, both by eminent scientists, suggest that the battle of the metaphors is already won, and the machine figure a thing of the past. To the layman listening to scientific discussions and reading scientific works today, it certainly does not seem so, except perhaps in physics, even though one knows to allow for the time-lag between the conclusions reached by great men and the general practice of the ranks of any discipline or profession. Thus we find Michael Polanyi in *The Logic of Liberty* saying, "Until the end of the nineteenth century, scientists believed implicitly in the mechan-

ical explanation of all phenomena. In the last fifty years, these premisses of science were abandoned, but not without causing considerable delay in the progress of discoveries which were inaccessible
from such premisses." Similarly, in Volume I of *Science and Civilisation in China*, Cambridge, 1954, Dr. Needham asks, "How was it that
Chinese backwardness in scientific theory co-existed with the
growth of an organic philosophy of Nature, interpreted in many
differing ways by different schools, but closely resembling that
which modern science has been forced to adopt after three centuries of mechanical materialism?"

What is the nature of this change of metaphor, actual or potential,
among scientists? Organic, non-mechanical—these are interesting
hints, in view of what we have already seen. But there are earlier
examples still, scientists again, who perhaps show more clearly
what may be happening. In 1937 Sir James Jeans, the astronomer
and physicist, says, "The universe begins to look more like a great
thought than a great machine." The tentative proposal of shift of
metaphor there, from machine to some form of thinking which is
obviously conceived of as *not* mechanical, is significant. Even more
so, because so unexpected, is something which Thomas Henry Huxley said in a scientific paper in 1856. This is the man who cham-
pioned the cause of Darwinism and who has come to seem almost
the embodiment of science in its most combative form. Yet it is
he who says, simply, "Nature is not a mechanism, she is a poem."
You may recall that Alfred Russell Wallace also compared nature
to a poem; he was writing poetry at that time, while Huxley here
speaks prose and the statement is to be found in his Scientific
Memoirs, if that seems to make it more reliable. In either case the
figure is the same. It is the final form of the nature-as-language metaphor, which in its turn was the final form of nature as method, in
human terms. That poets might turn to it seems predictable. That
scientists do so, agreeing apparently with Carlyle in *Heroes and
Hero-Worship* that "he who discerns nothing but Mechanism in the
Universe has in the fatalest way missed the secret of the Universe
altogether," is a good deal more singular. How do we interpret it?

Luckily we can at least be clear about one thing: this is not a
case of rejecting technology as such. Neither eminent scientists, nor

poets whatever name-calling may have gone on in this area, are Luddites or would-be machine-wreckers, ignorant and anachronistic. The machine is rejected by both not as fact but as metaphor; not as phenomenon but as methodology for thinking with.

IV

Good figures—as we have glimpsed with the help of poets and scientists—work. That is to say, they generate when in conjunction with the mind an energy-potential directed towards a particular discipline of interpretation. Work is what energy does. It is about all that we know about energy, fact, concept, figure or mystery as it is, observable in its consequences, uncomprehended as yet in its nature. Language has given it a name and thus suggested for it a speculative and complex unity; some would add, illusory. The question as to its nature and function lies behind much that we have been thinking about in this Chapter.

Whatever we may mean by it, the word has become one of the most central and topical in mid-twentieth-century thinking. "Energy" turns up everywhere, from the spots of intense radioactivity now known to be located in what are apparently empty spaces in the heavens, to the rhythmical waves and circuits which betoken waking or sleeping, health or sickness, in the human brain. Not merely does "energy" turn up everywhere, it turns out to be everything. If we can at all catch the vision of contemporary physics, we begin to apprehend as best we may that all matter, our own frames included, in this so solid-seeming universe consists in the last analysis only of charges and configurations of energy—whatever that may be.

Yet in this energetic cosmos of modernity, so beautifully figured or pre-figured by Blake and Wordsworth over 150 years ago, something curious seems to have happened to our figuring. It seems to me that when we imagine "energy" nowadays we have a strong tendency to do so in terms other than human.

Were you to ask most people today for an image of "energy," they would be likely to produce one of two, I believe: either the huge explosive boiling cloud which is atomic energy in the only form in which it has been made directly visible to the human eye, or else some great machine, perhaps one of the gigantic missiles of this decade, roaring sky- and space- and sunwards. In our generation such images of energy make any conceivable energy of the human mind-body organism appear paltry by comparison. We seem to be questioning the relevance or reality of human energy in the universe as we now see it. Can human energy have any connection with the energy of nuclear fission which is also, we are told, that of the sun and the flaming stars? Are not our technological artifacts vastly more powerful than we? (Yet perhaps never was there a generation which hungered more for energy, and in human terms. It is once again clearest among the young but it is not confined to them or to any one continent or culture. Our pursuit of energies only partially human in their isolation is an index of hunger—speed; sex; sports; crackpot causes and movements; the kinds of violence which, as has become clear, both individuals and communities prefer to a total absence of energy, to acquiescence in impotence.)

There is then natural energy, the energy of the machine, and the energy of the living organism and of that human body-mind in which, on this planet, the impetus of evolution appears to be embodied. Notice that we have here the three parts of the two basic metaphors for nature into which our original six figures were finally reduced. Do we figure nature as machine (which entails figuring mind, as part of nature, in the same way—witness much of the thought in behavioural psychology or modern neurology for instance) or nature as energetic living organism which in its most developed form of mind never loses its resemblance to the native adaptive originality of the lowliest organism, and whose tendency toward just such originality and adaptation is, if that vision can be trusted of which Teilhard de Chardin is the latest exponent, inherent in some way in matter itself—at which point we come back to energy again, if this is what matter is?

The scientists reject the nature-as-machine metaphor, not from prejudice but presumably because it is not exact enough and consequently will not work. For a fairly detailed discussion of it, may I refer the reader to *Personal Knowledge* where the comparison, specifically, of mind to machine is cast out because the energy the machine appears to possess is seen to be illusory unless it is implicitly supplemented by the unformalized tacit operations of the intelligence which decides what the machine is for and uses it for that purpose. A machine, however finely developed, must work in the last resort derivatively, being dependent on the groping figuring energy of the human mind. It is the latter which is eventually postulated as the metaphor for nature, not any form of automatism, no matter how advanced or seeming-wonderful.

Carlyle, the poet who raised the question of energy in connection with method, has something to say here. Indeed his essay, "Signs of the Times," from which we have already quoted, is a full-length discussion of this very point. Asserting that his age, our modern age, is best characterized as "the Age of Machinery, in every outward and inward sense of that word," he speaks out in his own way the point made by Michael Polanyi, "For man is not the creature and product of Mechanism; but, in a far truer sense, its creator and producer." Mind plus machine have very real powers of operation; but only mind with a different kind of formalized system such as a language has powers of fertile energy and divination. A machine does not have the right sort of energy for imaging nature.

Carlyle all through his work envisages nature and the cosmos as a great tissue of what he calls Force. "This Universe . . . is a Force, a thousandfold Complexity of Forces; a Force which is *not we* . . . Force, Force, everywhere Force; we ourselves a mysterious Force in the centre of that." This may sound like contradiction, yet it is not; it is simply the postulation of energy in nature and energy in the human mind, not identical the one with the other and hence capable of forming a metaphor. (You cannot, as you will realize, make a metaphor out of two things exactly alike.) Yet Carlyle insists that there is an energy in the mind, a Force. From this springs his whole gospel of "Work" which has, I think, been misunderstood insofar as it was taken to be preaching of sheer labour, for moral or edificatory reasons. Work is for this poet the result of man's mental energy, donated voluntarily, as he remarks in *Sartor Resartus,* as a counterpart to the great Energy which is nature. He says it perhaps most clearly in *Past and Present,* of 1843: "Labour is Life: from the inmost heart of the Worker rises his god-given Force, the sacred celestial Life-Essence . . . Man, Son of Earth and Heaven, lies there not in the innermost heart of thee a Spirit of active Method, a Force for Work?" And lest this force or energy might seem to be mechanical, he says a little later in the same work, "He that works, whatsoever be his work, he bodies forth thc form of Things Unseen; a small Poet every Worker is." The work which is the metaphoric counterpart of "this active universe," in Wordsworth's phrase, is not that of machine operating in apparent though illusory independence. It is that of mind-body organism working with its figures including itself. Only there, apparently, is there generated an energy speculative, groping, prefiguring and mysterious enough to image natural energy sufficiently exactly for the mind to be able to divine with it. Man: earth—two halves of the tally.

This is one of the major elements in the working of the human metaphor, and the method it implies. We shall go on now to watch it at work, in a simple and then in a more extended form. There will be a change of emphasis, too, from now on, and perhaps it may come as a relief. This Method we have been following, human though I have called it, may have seemed so far both academic and remote, a concern for the great, perhaps, but not for us. If so, that is over now. The man who is the tally is everyman, the earth is the world which is each man's work. All that is required is to be a conscious mind-body moving over the face (lovely anthropomorphic phrase) of the earth. Keats, when he too speaks of the native poet in every human being, adds two further requirements: that we be well-nurtured in our mother-tongue, and that we have learned to love. With this in mind, we can begin to look at the man/earth tally, the human metaphor, at work.

Three

UNIVERSE WITHIN AND WITHOUT

I

THE WORKING FIGURE FOR THE UNIVERSE, THE METHODOLOGY of interpretation, proposed by poets and now in process of legitimization by scientists, is that of organism; and in its finest form, not simply that of any organism but of the most complex, active and powerful, the organism which is at once body and mind and which expresses itself and extends itself through language. It is a struggle, still going on; a struggle forward, I believe, but also a reference back to what has been before—and this is true for our own enquiry. You may remember that in Chapter I we left Blake offering us his final insight: cities are men, mountains and rivers are men. If it sounded primitive to us then, we must revise our thinking. We are back, or have moved on, to anthropomorphic thought.

We have been educated into regarding anthropomorphic thinking as discredited and outworn superstition. It begins to appear that such a view, widespread as it is, is no longer realistic or serviceable, in the light of modern methods of thought and interpretation. Notice what seems to have happened to the notion or concept of "anthropomorphic thought," for we shall meet with other cases of the same thing: we have permitted those to define it who reject it *a priori* on mixed grounds of conscience, prejudice and ignorance; devoted solely to some other method, they cannot know the powers of this one, yet reject what they think they know of it. We have then taken this as a real definition and have felt obliged to follow suit. Again we can see how closely method and man's image of himself go together. For what you make of anthropormorphic thinking and figuring depends on what you really think is the *morphe* of *anthropos*, the form of man.

Much of what we saw in the last Chapter about method and the operation of the mind bears on this, and need only be remembered, not repeated, here. It should at least be clear by now that neither poets nor any other thinkers are arguing in favour of simplistic or sterile figures in this kind. There are bad metaphors and figures to hand. The best way of representing the Almighty is not as an old man with a beard, for instance, nor are the best lines in Milton those where he bids daffadillies fill their cups with tears. Bad or null metaphor, however, does not rule out metaphor itself. So too the ancient counterpoise of microcosm and macrocosm is probably best put from the mind at this point, the more so since we know so many of these figures in the rather frigid codified form in which they reached into, and died out in, the differing thought patterns of the Renaissance. Our best plan will be to go to the poets who used this form as a living method, in more modern times and in defiance of the antagonistic scientific method then prevailing. It is their defiance, based on a deeper insight than was current in their own time, which makes them able to help us now in ours.

Blake will be the first. We left him at the point where he was saying that cities are men ("Organisms, societies, human persons, not least, cities, are delicate devices for regulating energy and putting it to the service of life," Lewis Mumford, *The City in History*, 1961, p. 571), rivers and mountains are men—on which another poet shall comment later in this Chapter. When I quoted the passage before, however, I left it unfinished. The last line runs: "In every bosom a Universe expands as wings." All of Blake's extraordinary figuring in anthropomorphic terms, the red sun which is a globule of man's blood, the moment of time which is only really measurable as the pulsation of an artery, contributes to this thought of his, which, again in *Jerusalem*, he puts into the words, "and all you behold, though it appears Without, it is Within." Man, for Blake, is not man unless this interchange is working properly. Without it there arises a crisis, such as we have now, "Which separated the stars from the mountains, the mountains from Man / And left Man a little grovelling Root outside of Himself."

The poet who is most like Blake in his insistence on the human in thought and the human form as a methodology of interpretation is Goethe. He says in his Maxims (shrewdly when you think about it, and echoed now by certain scientists of our day, e.g., Max Knoll in *Man and Time* from the Eranos collection for 1957) that human thought is bound to be anthropomorphic or humanly-formed in any case—what else can it be?—and we would do better to work consciously along with this rather than try to persuade ourselves that we can think in some absolute non-human way. His own thinking, in natural history, is at times almost scandalously anthropomorphic. For instance, we find him telling one of his visitors that he thinks of the globe of the earth as a great living creature in its atmosphere, engaged in alternate breathing in and breathing out. The human form was so central to Goethe's thinking and research in science that we find him creating a physiological theory of colour in *Die Farbenlehre* in an attempt to counteract what he regarded as the excessively detached mathematical operations of Newtonian optics.

Like Blake, he does not end here. In words which might almost be a translation of one of Blake's phrases, Goethe says, in one of the *Gott, Gemüt und Welt* poems, "Im Innern ist ein Universum auch"—there is also a universe within. It is beautiful and fitting that this image should have been present when Goethe died. One of his many interlocutors during his life was present at his death and he recounts Goethe's last minutes, the noble dignity and beauty which were with him till the end, death when it came being little more than the laying back of his head in the comfortable armchair where he was seated. By inspiration the observer recalls and applies to him words from Faust: "And the breast which had called forth, borne and cherished a world within itself ceased to rise and fall." It is a wonderful epitaph for a man of Goethe's cast of thought.

A universe without and a universe within—is this not after all a mere survival of microcosm-macrocosm thinking, the establishment of static series and correspondences in that pattern-making which the Middle Ages loved? But thought has changed since then, and so has the relation between these two universes as our two poets saw it. First, the vision is dynamic; the two universes are not in fixed correspondence with one another, they are in a constant active interchange. Second, each interpenetrates the other. We have to avoid thinking in terms of contiguity, the two universes touching and meeting one another, as on the boundary of two nation-states, or the side-by-sideness of two bodies. I find my own mind is liable to take up an old-fashioned image here and suppose that a universe, or indeed any system, is actually separate, walled off somehow and insulated from other universes or systems or bodies. Only after thought does one realize how unreal a picture this is, even of everyday bodies and things. The world is not a collection of pill-like atoms, insulated bodies, isolated minds. It would, I believe, be nearer the truth as we at present see it to think of all organizations, even of matter, as open systems, astonishingly interpenetrated by other systems, open networks through which the other equally open networks of matter or mind or spirit, near or far, drift and work. This is not, as I am imaging it, an amorphous world, but a universe of open forms which interfuse or, in the original sense, influence one another.

If this is true of bodies, inanimate or animate, seeming so solid and well-skinned yet so open to external influences, from love to fallout, it is even more marked when the mind enters, for mind in an organism increases incalculably its capacity to "take things in," as the English phrase has it. Mind is one of the great devices for effecting the constant living interchange between the two universes. It is, besides being half of the Man/Earth figure, the locus of that figure's operation. Within the mind, then, the self-subsisting universe of that mind and the concomitant universe of all nature and all space may meet and—marry.

The image is Bacon's; and as we go on to meet it in other poets we may recognize it for what it is, one of the three basic metaphors, all bodily, by which we figure the relation of these two universes, their living intercourse. They are breathing, eating and mating; look for them in all the areas of man's life which matter most to him (say, in education or in religion). Thus do we make the openness of the bodily nature image the closest and most vital of mental or spiritual relations, and rightly so. It was in this way that Bacon, passionately interested as he was in revitalizing the relation between the intelligence of man and the natural world, images the meeting point of the two universes in the Great Instauration. It has to be a fusing, a making of two into one (almost as in metaphor itself), a living connection as against a static or dead arrangement, and it has to be fertile. So he speaks of "the bridal chamber of the Mind and the Universe" which it is his task to prepare, "out of which marriage let us hope (and be this the prayer of the bridal song) there may spring helps to men." The same image, and in this same context, is used by Novalis, Emerson, and centrally in the work of the poet in whose thought and work we are going to explore the relations between the two universes within and without: Wordsworth.

There is conceivable an ideal form of this figure—a state in which mind and nature would be as perfectly matched as, very rarely, two human beings can be in the mutual completing and interpreting at all levels of life which constitutes a near-perfect union between man and woman. On the more ordinary level, however, the figure as used by these poets and thinkers is interesting, because it changes in the two hundred years between Bacon's time and Wordsworth's. Perhaps this is not only because the relation of mind and nature to one another has changed, although that certainly would be the case; but also because, and not independently of the former cause, the concept of a marriage has changed too. A figure or metaphor of interpretation which involves an institution of society will both affect and be affected by the evolution of that institution in the course of everyday life. Blake, you remember, insists that marriage and love are intimately bound up with the work of the imagination. So does Novalis; so does Shaw in his astonishing connection of myth, love, and political economics in his discussion of "The Ring of the Nibelungs" in *The Perfect Wagnerite*, 1898.

Bacon sees the marriage of the Mind and the Universe, as he so admirably calls it, in a somewhat one-sided fashion. Only a Shakespeare probably could rise to the "marriage of true minds" and the strength, realism and tenderness of the view of marriage we glimpse, in its latest form, in *The Tempest*. Bacon's view of marriage was no doubt the prevailing one of his time, a one-sided domination of one party over the other. The mind, the male, is to assert its dominance, yet must minister to, as it subjugates, the partner, nature or the female, who in turn must bring forth progeny at the husband's will. The progeny in this case (forgive me if the metaphor takes a rather odd turn here) will be primarily technological. This is the mastery which Bacon sees and which he did his best to further.

With Wordsworth we have something very different. Simply in the course of history the concept of marriage has changed, the vision of the universe has changed, and Wordsworth uses this marital metaphor to emphasize mutual interpretation of mind and world rather than exertion of power by intellect over nature. He uses the metaphor in the lines which form the last part of the first Book of the uncompleted poem, *The Recluse*. They are often published as a preface to *The Excursion*. Wordsworth speaks of them as "a kind of Prospectus of the design and scope of the whole Poem"—that long philosophical poem which he always intended to write and never did. *The Prelude* indicates what it might have been, and to that poem Wordsworth gave the sub-title, "The Growth of a Poet's Mind." It is, therefore, in a context of psychological research that these lines are set:

> . . . the discerning intellect of Man,
> When wedded to this goodly universe
> In love and holy passion . . .

The poet sees this marriage as still in the future, and adds for himself the aspiration:

> I, long before the blissful hour arrives,
> Would chant, in lonely peace, the spousal verse
> Of this great consummation.

It is very reminiscent of Bacon, and that is good, for Wordsworth knew and loved his great predecessor, and we in our turn can see here once again the dynasty of the poets at work. (In these lines Wordsworth claims descent from Milton, and invokes Shakespeare also.) It is the differences, however, that we shall look at more closely.

The nature of the marriage between mind and universe, as Wordsworth sees it, is described a few lines later.

> ... my voice proclaims
> How exquisitely the individual Mind
> (And the progressive powers perhaps no less
> Of the whole species) to the external World
> Is fitted:—and how exquisitely, too,
> Theme this but little heard of among Men,
> The external World is fitted to the Mind;
> And the creation (by no lower name
> Can it be called) which they with blended might
> Accomplish:—this is our high argument.

The simplicity of this passage, all too rare among prospectuses of modern works on psychological research, might be a model for any precise and careful statement of scientific purpose. Yet its openness should not blind us to its grasp and range. The marriage of Mind and external World is seen no longer as the domination of one by the other, but the interpenetration of two systems, who are to achieve by their "blended might"—in contrast to the concept of mind subjugating nature, and, one surmises, much more healthily, whether in interpretation of universe or the institution of marriage —something which the poet calls "creation." The marriage is to be fruitful, as is proper, but the fruitfulness is not thought of in the same terms as those of Bacon, who saw the offspring as "helps to men," engines of thought such as he tried to construct in *Novum Organum* or engines as such in his Mechanical Arts. Wordsworth speaks only of a creation, and marvels at, yet re-emphasizes his term as he goes by it, showing he knew what he was doing, and meant his vision of the fertile and mutual interaction of mind and external world to be grasped as a metaphor of the whole Creation, the immense active process which poets have always sensed, and which we moderns have become so greatly interested in again, through rival theories in scientific cosmogony in the past few years.

Universe and mind are fitted to each other, and create the one the other. The term "fitted" may mislead us again, suggesting as it does a puzzle pattern fitting with its counterpart, unless we remember to go beyond this sense back into the marriage metaphor. When we say of a couple that they are "suited" to one another, which is this sense of "fitted," we mean something much more dynamic and growing than a mere agreement of set shapes, of personality or behaviour. In such a marriage there is a creation of each by other (Soloviev, the Russian theologian, writes of this somewhere) as well as the creation of the family. In this sense the Universe creates the Mind, the Mind the Universe, in what Poe, in that strange starry essay where he investigates this very process, *Eureka,* calls "reciprocity of adaptation."

That the external world does move towards mind has become clearer to us through the development of evolutionary thought. This was already well under way when Wordsworth began his investigation into the nature of the mind, and it is interesting to see how he takes the trouble, in that prospectus of his, to insert this point of view, the progressive powers of the whole species. The external world also, Wordsworth says, creates the individual mind. We pass here from what Renan called "an embryogeny of the human spirit" to the developmental life history of the individual mind. This is of course what Wordsworth was following out in *The Prelude,* using himself for the subject of his enquiry. He examines here, with particular emphasis on childhood, the moulding, figuring, stimulating and nourishing of the mind by the works of nature, both as the child grows and after adulthood if the said adult chooses to continue the process and to go on changing and being changed in a constant interaction with whatever "Nature" he or she may be surrounded by; not lapsing, as it seems that many do, into what Wordsworth calls the sleep of death of the sensual.

I put Nature in that last sentence in quotes because it does not cover simply green hills and waters and vegetation. I do not want to make Wordsworth, or any true poet, sound like a Back-to-the-Land man. If you were brought up, as I was for part of my childhood, in a big city you will know what I mean; for a child this becomes his nature also, in the double sense—the interesting smell and texture of tar melting on roads in summer heat, the small dark shop where they sold rough hand-carved wooden toys, the superb pattern of struts and stays on the river's suspension bridges. Wordsworth knows this—you can see it in his sonnet on Westminster Bridge—so that what he is considering here is not the effect of rural nature on the mind, but the effect of environment in general when used as a continual tally and means of growth in the self-interpretation of the developing mind. In the wonderful passage on the baby's gradual awakening into consciousness in Book II of *The Prelude*, he says that the mind (again using the same terms he has used before)

> Creates, creator and receiver both,
> Working but in alliance with the works
> Which it beholds.

There is a sense also in which the individual mind creates the universe. I do not want to get involved with philosophy, but simply at the level of physiology it has become clear from modern research into perception that the senses of the body do not record mechanically or automatically, but shape and build up wholes, as if they were artists from the beginning. The exhibition of this process was one of the great contributions of Gestalt psychology. This is all part of the "fittingness" which Wordsworth talks about. The mutual creation of mind and universe in blended might is, however, something more than this. It would, I think, cover in Wordsworth's thought every form taken by man's active shaping spirit; all the seven dynasties and all the work upon society and, in this poet very particularly, all the humble works of unnamed multitudes of simple men and women and children. Yet at this level just as much as at any other, the growth and activity depend on mind and universe together, never singly but in marriage. We are not conditioned automatically by our environment, nor can this creation go on in a mind alone, insulated against its surroundings.

It is the mind that Wordsworth himself is particularly interested in, not as the would-be dominator but as the counterpart of the external world. The question arises therefore for him as for every psychological investigator: how can one examine the mind? In this prospectus of his he had spoken earlier of "the individual Mind that keeps her own inviolate retirement." Must one attempt to break in and rifle that secret place? Wordsworth, and other poets who are also interested in this form of research, indicate not. He suggests another method, seeming at first fanciful perhaps, yet when looked at more closely of extraordinary interest. It was not new—I think the poets have always worked this way—but his emphasis was new, and he realized this. Hence that interesting little comment which he inserts in the passage quoted on p. 82. "Theme this but little heard of among Men." He goes on to identify this theme as the exquisiteness of the external world's fitting to the mind. As far as I understand this, I take it to mean an affirmation of the man/earth tally as an essential method of psychological investigation. The workings of the human mind are best observed, perhaps can be observed only, in alliance with the works of nature. This is the converse of the great metaphor we were considering in the last Chapter. If scientists and poets seem to be progressing towards some agreement in our time that the most fitting operative metaphor for nature is mind, Wordsworth here affirms, methodologically also, the same figure the other way round. Only as universe will you understand the mind.

A Universe—that was Bacon's term, and Goethe's. Yet Wordsworth's careful "external World" may perhaps be better, for it is more explicit. When we think of a universe within, we may be tempted to imagine some vast shapeless pseudo-cosmos of our own conceiving, and perhaps for this reason Wordsworth warns us off this, back into the cosmos as given. The universe, the external world, the earth, are our means for comprehending the mind, in the poetic method. Not some chimeric universe but the one we have been given is the figure, which is to say, the instrument of research.

II

If the whole universe is a field of figures by which to begin to interpret and grasp the structure of the mind, the range of possibilities here is almost infinite. So too are the examples of this work going on in the works of the poets. In order not to lose our way we shall stay mainly with *The Prelude,* at the same time allowing its figures to remind us of similar ones in other poets. This poem is one of the great storehouses of working figures of this sort, and is particularly valuable since a number of them are used consciously as mind-images, and there are passages also of commentary on the method itself.

Book I begins with just such an image:

> For I, methought, while the sweet breath of Heaven
> Was blowing on my body, felt within
> A corresponding mild creative breeze,
> A vital breeze which travelled gently on
> O'er things which it had made, and is become
> A tempest, a redundant energy
> Vexing its own creation. 'Tis a power
> That does not come unrecognized, a storm
> Which breaking up a long-continued frost
> Brings with it vernal promises . . .

The wind in the outside universe is answered by an inner energy, figured by a breeze which yet is "creative," travels across "things which it had made" and vexes "its own creation." Three times within this brief passage Wordsworth harks back to his idea that external and internal universe create at their blending point. After the metaphor of breeze we move on to storm, i.e., weather in a larger context, and then to a change of season. We have already mentioned the fundamental breathing and air figure; it is so common that examples from poets are unnecessary.

Now another figure from *The Prelude:*

Caverns there were within my mind, which sun
Could never penetrate, yet did there not
Want store of leafy arbours where the light
Might enter in at will.

Here are landscapes, above and below ground, differentiated in
this case by the difference of their lighting. The mind needs images
both light and dark for its varied workings; a poet of the first is
Valéry who employs for his figures sun, sea and the diamond; of the
second, Novalis, with his preference for night and for mine-work-
ings. We shall be returning to caverns in The Prelude's imagery
shortly with a grander example. For the moment it is enough to
begin to consider landscape, preliminarily, in this way. If you are
thinking of landscape (or even perhaps the mind) as static, may I
remind you, as I am reminding myself, that it is no such thing? It is
always in process of change, slow or vast; and in addition its considerable sweep or variety of structures lends itself well to what
Emerson calls the metamorphosis between inner and outer. In Book
II of The Prelude Wordsworth says, "And what I saw / Appear'd
like something in myself, a dream, / A prospect in my mind." All
earthly landscapes are potentially prospects in the mind (dream
landscapes are necessarily so, of course.) Indeed I believe that no
earthly landscape is fully possessed by us until something of this
metamorphosis has been set in operation. Landscapes which have
not been worked on and assimilated in such a way remain sterile
monologue, left lonely or possessed not by the thinking and creating
mind in every man but only by the financial power of tourist trade
and travel agent. I feel that an example would be the American
West whose staggering size and drama has not yet really entered
our consciousness, so that we do not know what prospects in the
mind are correlated not only with massive toothed fields of black
pinnacles of broken rock in white sand—these are more ordinary
and form merely the outer edges,—but with desert pavemented over
hundreds of square inhuman miles with salmon-pink and copper-
sulphate-blue, or with aeons of our stratified crust racked by huge
splits so deep they become black at once as if opening into the
Antipodean night, with edges as hard and dark as old sword

wounds. Even the little I have seen of its immensity makes the imagination ask, "What is going on here?" and look inside itself as well as outside, as Wordsworth did continually:

> Vast prospect of the world which I had been
> And was.

The mind needs such images for itself. T. E. Lawrence has made some beginning on desert imagery for us, in another place, but this incredible country awaits its poet, and so is not yet fully ours. How much of this lies behind the drive towards exploration, and the reading of travel books, it is hard to say; probably a good deal.

The landscape may be desert; it may be mountains and valleys. "O the mind, mind has mountains; cliffs of fall / Frightful, sheer, no-man-fathomed," Hopkins writes, towards the end of the nineteenth century; and already the fifteenth-century anonymous English poet of that masterpiece of meditation on human and divine love, *Quia Amore Langueo*, spoke of being "In a vaile of restless minde." In the diary of Paul Klee, the artist, there is an entry, in 1900, "The comparison of my spirit with the different moods of the landscape is a frequent preoccupation of mine. My personal and poetic way of apprehending landscape lies at the root of this." Then, after meditating on the simile, he moves straight into the metaphor: "It is autumn. Mists go creeping along the river of my soul." Or the prospect may be green and growing. Keats explores such a one in, most fittingly, the *Ode to Psyche*, "some untrodden region of my mind" where there are hills and valleys, and "branchéd thoughts" grow instead of pine trees; that is wild nature, and then, too, there is the garden nature of this landscape, "the wreath'd trellis of a working brain, / With buds, and bells, and stars without a name." The human spirit imaged by vegetation is present in Hopkins, "Send my roots rain!" or George Herbert in the seventeenth century,

> "Who would have thought my shrivel'd heart
> Could have recovered greennesse? It was gone
> Quite underground; as flowers depart
> To see their mother-root, when they have blown . . .

And now in age I bud again,
After so many deaths I live and write . . .

(The Flower)

These are just random instances, and they lead back to *The Prelude* again and to Wordsworth characterizing in this image the whole nature of our inner being:

Hush'd, meanwhile,
Was the under soul, lock'd up in such a calm
That not a leaf of the great nature stirr'd.

(Book III)

The great nature—Wordsworth knows well what he is about.

After these preliminary examples, we will turn now to the three great figures which occur through *The Prelude,* each time in connection with the imagination, explicitly. In these three, Wordsworth figures the mind as underground river, as gulf or abyss, and as stars.

In the final book of the poem, where Wordsworth is summing up and taking leave of his own research into the nature of the mind, he compares the latter to a river, flowing partly above ground and partly below. He speaks here of the great central activity of mind, calling it Imagination and saying that it has been his theme all through the poem. It is rather typical of a poet that he announces his theme at the end of his work rather than at the beginning.

What Wordsworth calls the Imagination proves to be the mind itself, in its most active and shaping form. He mentions love and intellect as parts of it, and goes on to say that imagination itself is "but another name for absolute strength / And clearest insight, amplitude of mind, / And reason in her most exalted mood." (Here is another poet insisting on the central unity of all the powers of the mind.) He then develops his thought, in this context which is central to the whole poem and the investigation contained in it:

This faculty hath been the moving soul
Of our long labour: we have traced the stream
From darkness, and the very place of birth

In its blind cavern, whence is faintly heard
The sound of waters; follow'd it to light
And open day, accompanied its course
Among the ways of Nature, afterwards
Lost sight of it bewilder'd and engulph'd,
Then given it greeting, as it rose once more
With strength, reflecting in its solemn breast
The works of man and face of human life,
And lastly from its progress have we drawn
The feeling of life endless, the great thought
By which we live, Infinity and God.

A river as an image of human life in any form seems trite enough. Its trickle of a beginning, the gradual growth in size and power, the broad smooth urbanized middle reaches, the final merging with the infinite sea—every poet must have made use of it, from Shakespeare down to very prosaic poets indeed, and it seems to us that there is little to work with here until we realize that when we think in those terms we are not thinking of a river at all but of a concept, the class of things covered by the word "river." One does not see rivers like that, spread out from source to sea-mouth. When one recalls "river," what has one seen? I think particularly of the six-year-old who was myself, watching in silence and awe the colossal spread of the Brahmaputra which we were shortly to cross by ferry; much later, standing on "le pont d'Avignon" whose nursery-rhyme presence had been familiar since childhood but which had given no warning of the nature of the river here, the Rhone flowing with a quiet and terrific speed all across its broad length—how proper it seemed to discover that in local church iconography the Rhone when it is to be represented appears as a bull; the same dash, the same overwhelming ponderousness, equally lethal. A river is particular, and it is with such figures, Blake's Minute Particulars, Mallarmé's exactitude, that work can be done. Once this is clear, we can look at Wordsworth's.

First, where it comes from: a murmuring spring invisible at first and only to be heard. Springs are certainly never banal. We do not search passionately and over long periods for the sources of the

Nile out of mere curiosity; we are exploring the upper reaches of
the mind, as presumably we are also doing in mountain climbing.
I know well only two springs; one, a tiny bubbling circle of water
in a cup of sand, by the side of a Sussex lane where we went for
walks as children; the other, the source of the Cam, which, dull
little river though it is, rises astonishingly, for it comes out from
under a shelf of stone from eight or ten springs at once, and is a
full-grown river as soon as born. Two quite different figures are
here, for minds envisaged differently: the child's spirit, perhaps,
or some continually renewed youth and innocence, and the birth
of the human race who as soon as they appeared, at least to judge
by the evidence of the caves whence they sprang, were fully man
—a river from the start. Wordsworth's river makes its way to light,
pursues its course (notice how ordinary a metaphor that is) and
then goes underground again for a while.

This is no leap of fantasy, but again, observation of particulars.
Much of the north of England is limestone country, and it is there
that such things happen. A river will vanish into the ground only
to re-emerge perhaps miles away, known by markers as the same
river yet making its way underground all that distance.

Wordsworth starts us off in a cavern. To the caverns we return
later, or repeatedly; and if you think of the river as a whole, the
total action of the mind seen as a simultaneity, then there is always
some part of it underground. It is an astonishing figure for the
mind's relation with its bodily structure, and for what we have
come to call, so unfortunately I believe, the unconscious or sub-
conscious. The mind flows through the caverns of the body. It is
diffused through the body as water on its tables and channels and
veins is diffused through the earth. The earth is, of course, a constant and unfailing figure for the body; the external to the external,
hills and landscape and geography seen, as many a poet has seen
them, as body-forms; or the sombre beauty of *Memento, homo,
quia pulvis es* of which Catholics are ceremonially reminded once
a year. We are dust, we remember. But it is not merely a matter of
identity of substance or comparison of external structure. There
is the inwardness also, and here caves and all that is within the
earth are supremely important for figuring the essentially dark and

mysterious inwardnesses, bodily or mental, of ourselves. All mine-working, as Novalis expresses in *Heinrich von Ofterdingen,* all pot-holing and speleology is a discovering of the inward structures of body and mind, and beyond that lie less investigable powers again, the great forces which heat up the working centres of mountains we have tunnelled through, the massive shifts and faultings which tremor our sanity, the blazing centre. Possibly if the eighteenth century had been less insistent on the rational, the Lisbon earthquake and tidal wave would not have seemed quite so preternatural. The mind has such impulses, no less than the crust of the world, if you do not batten them down or avert your eyes.

The stream, in Wordsworth, issues from such darkness. Very exactly he speaks of birth—for this is not its beginning. Neither mind nor stream starts with its visible birth into the light of day. What cavern life the mind led in the womb we have yet to imagine, but it is recognized and indicated here at least. It returns to other caverns after a time. Wordsworth's own poem, which we might expect to find commenting formally on the form of its subject matter, returns also on itself in the middle, in the books called *Retrospect —Imagination How Impaired and How Restored.* These are the periods known to all of us when the activity of the mind dives inwards and seems to disappear from sight. We tend at present to use the dreadful metaphor of "block" for this not infrequent human experience; indeed, "writer's block" has become a technical, almost a clinical term. Wordsworth's image is a far more fruitful, hopeful, and as I believe from practical experience here, more exact indication of what is happening during such times. The underground waters are the cave and lifespring of the spirit, and it returns there for a season to re-emerge, as Wordsworth says, with strength.

It may be that another poet, or poem, has been haunting you while we were looking at Wordsworth's. For Coleridge's *Kubla Khan* is surely another map of this same water and spirit. That sacred river, Alph, suggesting the beginning, runs partly above ground and partly below; it is rather hard to tell from the poem whether we are above or below ground at any particular stage, as maybe Coleridge found it hard to tell in his own mental life.

There is an outer landscape here too, furnished with greenery and natural beauties, but it is the inner which catches and holds: the progress through the caverns which, for this poet, were "measureless to man"—as notable an image for the mind as the bottomless lakes which we insist on believing in despite the pretensions of practical men that they have taken their sounding—dropping to a sunless sea, a lifeless ocean to which the underground river sinks at last in tumult. (Coleridge's vision has far more of death in it than Wordworth's does.) There is a spring here too where the sacred river is cast up to view, but compared with Wordsworth's whispering advent this one is violent and terrifying—a monstrous fountain more like a geyser, bursting out in fierce breaths which throw the boulders about as if they were pebbles, a pulsing exhalation which utters sounds like the ancient and still-to-come history of all mankind," ancestral voices prophesying war." Wordsworth heard these too, in winds among the rocks in his native Westmorland, "sounds that are / The ghostly language of the ancient earth." There are figures, it seems, among the sounds of earth as well as among its sights. In *Kubla Khan* it is one of the superb touches that the sunny pleasure dome with caves of ice, the palace of the mind which is compounded at once of natural material and human artifice, is set midway between the fountain and the caves and hears the music equally of each. (Since human artifice is admitted as a part of nature in this figuring, as it should be, not least of the modern delights of reading *Kubla Khan* in this method is to recall Dr. Needham's reference, *Science and Civilisation in China,* Vol. III, to a Chinese scientist who was at first "engaged under Khubilai Khan in hydraulic engineering works." Anyone who supposes such a reference might run counter to Coleridge's poem knows nothing of the nature of engineering or of the mind.)

Wordsworth's second explicit image for the mind, under its central function which he calls Imagination, is that of gulf or abyss. He uses this three times at least; once in the "Prospectus" we have already looked at, and twice in *The Prelude.* The first example finds him speaking of the gulf of Chaos and Old Night, which Milton traversed in his visionary journey as a poet in *Paradise Lost.* This is interesting, for it shows Milton, and Dante his epic traveller-ancestor, as an explorer of the mind. Each of these two poets was figuring the mind under the theological figures of his day; roomy landscapes they were too. Wordsworth turns to nature, but the gulf remains the same; "I must tread on shadowy ground," we find him saying, "must sink/ Deep," (how the separation of that mono-syllable falls away under the feet, so that we plunge with our guide!) "and aloft ascending, breathe in worlds/ To which the heaven of heavens is but a veil." He goes on a few lines later:

> Not Chaos, not
> The darkest pit of lowest Erebus,
> Nor aught of blinder vacancy—scooped out
> By help of dreams, can breed such fear and awe
> As fall upon us often when we look
> Into our Minds, into the Mind of Man,
> My haunt, and the main region of my Song.

That main region presents itself now, to the enquirer, as some pit where he can cling to the edge of the cliff and look over, knowing, if he is a poet, that he has to venture out into it.

Until the last thirty years, the only gulfs which man could know were to be seen from edges of cliffs and tops of mountains. Now that flying is a comparatively common human experience, we come to a whole new range of figures for just this exploration. Shelley was in some sense a precursor of it—such a flying and airborne poet, and there are beginnings of it perhaps in Saint-Exupéry, though mostly this figuring is still to be done. Meantime, Words-worth has his feet on his cliff edge; but the figure, and the fear, are the same.

A gulf suggests vast depth, danger, and a place of mystery where something is going on. Something works in true gulfs, be they mael-stroms or valleys so vast the atmosphere thicks up in them, or chasms between the alarming mantling energies of cumulo-nimbus glimpsed by moonlight through your jet's prism of a window. Wordsworth, in the next example, is at the peak of an Alpine pass —no mean eminence, the more so since he reached it on foot—and he describes what figured itself there before him:

Imagination—here the Power so called
Through sad incompetence of human speech,
That awful Power rose from the mind's abyss
Like an unfathered vapour that enwraps,
At once, some lonely traveller.

The mind is partly a place of enormous scope, a vacancy which is
there not for its own sake but in order that energies immanent in
the earth may have more play. (Did you notice how in the first
passage it is part of the function of dreams to "scoop out" this
vacancy yet deeper—what an astonishing image, and what a figure
for thinking about dreams with!) The rising of what seems something out of nothing, dangerous, blinding often, unformed as yet—
here is another image for how the mind works. Wordsworth in-
tensifies this image in the last book of *The Prelude*. After a long
foggy climb up the mountain by night, he and a few companions
emerge at last above the mist into the moonlight, to find themselves
companioned by the tops of hill after hill, and able now to see that
the mist is not spread over-all. There is a great rift in it, which
the poet describes thus:

through a rift—
Not distant from the shore on which we stood,—
A fixed, abysmal, gloomy breathing-place,
Mounted the roar of waters, torrents, streams,
Innumerable, roaring with one voice!
Heard over earth and sea and in that hour,
For so it seemed, felt by the starry heavens.

In the earlier version of this poem Wordsworth had added to that
scene the lines:

in that breach
Through which the homeless voice of waters rose,
That deep dark thoroughfare, had nature lodg'd
The Soul, the Imagination of the whole.

A dark abysmal breathing-place—breath of "spirit" which means "breath," or breath of body, or both, just as Coleridge's fountain of the mind pulsed out of the earth,—this is Wordsworth's second vision of the mind. This example seems to tie together all the three main images he is using, for the waters are here, unseen under their cloak of mist yet uttering their voices, and the great gulf of the working mind is here; and so is his third image, the starry heavens.

The last image for the mind, is, when we stop to look at it, of even vaster scope; for now the poet figures the working mind by the cosmos as a whole. It was vast enough in Wordsworth's day. Every extension of the history of the universe and of our earth, in time and space, extends the scope of this figure, without altering its validity. Indeed it has been suggested to me[1] that space exploration in our day is, seen in another light than the exhilarating scientific or the depressing political one, another chapter in man's ever-outward (or should I say inward?) exploration of himself. Walt Whitman had visions of this in his wonderful poem of 1871, *Passage to India,* where the at first terrestrial passage becomes a launching out into the universe as well as into "primal thought," the soul, and God. Wordsworth in his concluding section of *The Prelude* draws an explicit likeness between mind and that landscape of stars above earth as he had described it earlier: "the express/ Resemblance of that glorious faculty/ Which higher minds bear with them as their own." The whole passage in which he develops this figure is too long to quote here, but it includes motion and rest, power, influences and lights sent forth and voices (i.e., language in some sense), creative renewal and the capacity of mind, as of universe, to "send abroad/ Kindred mutations," fresh luminaries, fresh forms and ideas. Whitman joins Wordsworth here too, speaking of God, the centre alike of universe and soul, as "shedding forth universes." Poe's universe of stars in *Eureka* is seen in much the same way, pulsating in alternations of creation and collapse.

It is no wonder that numerous poets turn to this, the grandest figure available to us, as the best image of the marriage of mind

[1] By Mr. Anthony Sirignano.

and nature. Wordsworth, Poe and Whitman we have mentioned. Mallarmé is not to be forgotten with *Un Coup de Dés,* in which poem he images mind, and universe, under the figure of dice, as a struggle between skill and chance, as it were; the poem on its last pages takes the configuration (in its typography on the page as well as in its subject matter) of a constellation of stars, as the dice, or thoughts, or stars, roll down the page or the mind or the sky to come to rest at last in some final sum-total, their consummate and sacred form as he says, arrived at definitively after passage through the mutability of mere accident. And if Mallarmé emphasizes the universe's trend towards formative order which is also that of thought, another poet whose long poem, *An Essay on Man,* is full of sudden leaps into the starry heavens will in his turn emphasize also the inherent chaos, of which the heavens also exhibit plenty. Pope says,

> This light and darkness in our chaos join'd
> What shall divide? The God within the mind.

His image may go half unnoticed, the more so since it occurs in the context of a discussion of moral virtue, a mere trite separation of black from white, as we say. But look at it again, and it is no such thing. It is the mind figured as a chaos of light and darkness awaiting the ordering of Creative Power as the formless void waited in the story in the Book of Genesis, Chapter I. What is more, this separation and ordering have to be accomplished over and over again. It is continuous, for no God within the mind, however we or that subtle and profound eighteenth-century genius may construe the phrase, can divide light from darkness in our minds or in our consciences once for all. It has to be done constantly, and so this figure envisages creation constantly renewed, as Wordsworth did, you remember, in the passage we started from, that creation which the two partners of the marriage accomplish with blended might: "This is our high argument." The fact that he says "our" and not "my" is interesting, as if he was aware of the poets' company at this working point.

This is one of the reasons why this star figure is so good; it provides nearly limitless resources for figuring the mind as energy and

void, order either provisional or reasonably assured ("constant as
the northern star"), and the working chaos of whole regions or
bodies. It provides for a due allowance of necessary order and necessary chaos and necessary emptiness within the mind, thus figured. The universe, seen in this way, is, as Wordsworth's gulf was,
a working-place. Thus all astronomy—great star pictures from
Mount Palomar, the plotting of radio-stars going on in China or
Russia or at Jodrell Bank, the current rival theories of the origins
of the universe, whether in some single explosive burst or in "continuous creation"—these are for poets figures for investigation of
the mind, its fixed or shifting forms, its relationships and spaces,
clouds, chaos, clusters, the explosions, vestiges of former powers,
the streamers of tangential and eccentric illumination, the steady
centres, shining and meditating as Mallarmé says, "brillant et
méditant." These, like the landscapes and gulfs, mountain streams
and bell-flowers (and the animalcules no less, according to the biologist Adolf Portmann in the *Man and Time* Eranos collection for
1957—"the exploration of the unconscious—and all work in biology
is ultimately such an exploration") are ourselves, seen in figure and
hence interpretable as we can never be in the direct immediacy of
our existence.

III

Having seen something of the extent and application of this aspect of the human metaphor, we need now to pause and take stock
briefly, for certain elements in our thinking today may stand in the
way of recognizing it for what it is, a method of speculation and
research. The two methodological difficulties come under the names
of "mysticism" and "pathetic fallacy." After we have looked at
those, we shall need to think of the method in terms of a psychology, and the meanings, not necessarily either helpful or relevant,
which that word tends to conjure up in contemporary minds.

We begin with "mysticism," the most widespread and probably
the most important of these red herrings. The word alone is an
agent of such confusion that we had better take concrete examples

if we are to see what is at stake here. One shall be from a poet, one from a scientist to keep us in balance, and both already familiar in this inquiry already. The poet is Wordsworth, the scientist Dr. Needham.

Wordsworth is a good case in point because he is a master of the human metaphor in many or all of its forms, and for that very reason is haunted by this label of "mysticism." Even Coleridge in one of his more unhelpful moments applies it to Wordsworth, in Chapter XXII of *Biographia Literaria:* "and without his strong sense, his *mysticism* would become *sickly*—mere fog and dimness!" (The italics are in the original.) Yet when Wordsworth comes to consider and state his own method, as he does in Book II of *The Prelude* (he uses the word "research" for what he is doing, as we shall see in a moment) he affirms the human metaphor as we have so far seen it—the interpretation of mind by natural phenomena— rejects as unsuitable what we think of as scientific method, but throws out even more determinedly any notion of mysticism at all.

> But who shall parcel out
> His intellect by geometric rules,
> Split, like a province, into round and square? . . .
> Who that shall point, as with a wand, and say,
> "This portion of the river of my mind
> Came from yon fountain? . . ."
> Hard task to analyse a soul, in which,
> Not only general habits and desires,
> But each most obvious and particular thought,
> Not in a mystical and idle sense,
> But in the words of reason deeply weigh'd,
> Hath no beginning.

The rejection of scientific method with its mathematical precision and analysis is not hostile. The fact that it is represented here by geometry makes that plain, for this was a branch of study to which this poet was in fact much devoted, as various references in *The Prelude* make plain, particularly the great Stone and Shell dream in Book V, where the Stone is Euclid and one of mankind's two greatest treasures. It is rejected as unadapted to this psychological subject matter which is peculiar in being a total continuum in motion and also, both originally and in the detail of its behaviour moment by moment, without ascertainable beginnings. The metaphor of the river is introduced instead, and the assumption on which this is based is then characterized, not as "mystical and idle" but as founded upon reason. Yet, given this pair, reason is as difficult of definition as is mysticism, which brings us to our second example, where a scientist wrestles with the two. This is Dr. Needham on the Tao, in Section 10 of Volume II of *Science and Civilisation in China.*

The theme, of great interest in itself, of this part of the work is that a certain type of mysticism can be more favourable to the advance of scientific knowledge than a certain type of rationalism. The pair of concepts, or words, appear explicitly,[2] and the two bents of mind are examined in the mystical Taoists and the rationalist Confucians. The author begins by telling us that Taoism has been largely misunderstood in the past:

> Taoist religion has been neglected and Taoist magic has been written off wholesale as superstition, Taoist philosophy has been interpreted as pure religious mysticism and poetry, the scientific or 'proto'-scientific side of Taoist thought has been very largely overlooked, and the political position of the Taoists still more so . . . Taoism was religious and poetical, yes; but it was also at least as strongly magical, scientific, democratic and politically revolutionary. (pp. 34 ff.)

We halt here between a grand and appetite-whetting vision of the Tao, working in no less than five dynasties and implying a view of unity between them, and a shadow of divisions already at work somewhere, in the implied opposing of "pure religious mysticism and poetry" and "religious and poetical" on the one hand, and science on the other . Such slight verbal clues would not be enough

2 Cf. the sentence on p. 77, for instance: "The question may then be asked, under what social conditions do mysticism and rationalism have respectively the role of progressive social forces?"

to base any discussion on; but following through the next forty pages, on the relation between Taoist nature-mysticism and science, one comes upon the divisions being dug plainly, and difficulties with both "mysticism" and "reason." To take the former first, Dr. Needham draws a line dividing mysticism into two kinds, one in his view beneficent, the other not.

There is of course a great distinction between the mystical naturalism with which this section is concerned, and other forms of mysticism which are focused in purely religious concentration upon a God or gods. All that the former characteristically asserts is that there is much in the universe which transcends human reason here and now, but since it prefers the empirical to the rational, it adds that the sum total[3] of incomprehensibility will diminish if men humbly explore the occult properties and relations of things. Religious mysticism (in the usual sense) is very different; it dotes upon the arbitrary residuum and seeks to minimise or deny the value of investigations of natural phenomena.   (p. 97)

The first sort of mysticism, which is for Dr. Needham one of the principal notes of Taoist thought, friendly to science and not unfriendly to reason though with a tendency to bypass it, might perhaps be identified outright with poetry[4] (allowing us to dispense with the word "mysticism" in this case); poetry recognized as a heuristic discipline, on good terms with science and fulfilling rather than denying reason, as Wordsworth maintains. We should be left then with Dr. Needham's second sense of the word, religious mysticism which opposes science and is mystery-mongering and "obscurantist"—he adds that very term in a footnote a little later.

Religious mysticism is not our concern here; indeed, I believe, not the concern of the poet, as such, at all. The poet and the mystic are

---

[3] Notice the odd arithmetical metaphor, applying "sum total," "diminish" and "residuum" to the incomprehensible in the universe. Exception made for highly technical mathematical operations on an infinite series, the metaphor implies that the unknown is finite.

[4] Dr. Needham himself, in Section 11, speaks of "the Taoist poetry and vision."

distinct, to half-echo Keats for a moment, and each belongs in his own discipline or dynasty.[5] What does matter to poetry is the absence or presence of a spirit of faction between the dynasties themselves, such a spirit as is implicit in the poet's "mystical and idle," explicit in the scientist's "obscurantist." Hostile though they may be in their turn to science as Dr. Needham complains, and to poetry as well (a very wise friend of mine, a priest, once recommended me never to read Thomas à Kempis because his views on the imagination are unfit for poets), it is possible to think of the mystics as engaged in heuristic in their turn, religious mysticism taking on, from this point of view, the aspect of a specialized method of enquiry into an area of the universe of experience which can be explored in no other way and which is also the field of one of humanity's oldest and deepest preoccupations. There is considerable irony in the willingness of scientists nowadays to admit as practically respectable such human preoccupations as magic and astrology, if religion is to be excluded from the amnesty from the beginning.

It brings us back in the end to what is reasonable, to what is the nature of the rational, of rationalism, of human reason. With this word, as with mysticism, Dr. Needham has difficulty, and here, too, makes a distinction. Footnote b, p. 97, of this same volume provides a comment on, and an alternative for, the word "rationalism" as used in the argument:

> My friend Mr. S. Adler questions whether 'formalism' would not be a better word here. Rationalist systems sometimes leave room for a measure of non-rationalisable arbitrariness ('the illogical core of the universe'). The real contrast would then be between formalised orthodoxy and liberal open-mindedness.

It would indeed.

If we need pursue mysticism no further, we are still left with

---

[5] Not all poets think this. For a recent statement of the opposing view, cf. Elizabeth Jennings, *Every Changing Shape*, London, 1961. This work, which starts from the premise that poetry and mysticism are closely related, gives in its first chapter a good account of the muddle which the term "mysticism" is currently in.

reason, appealed to by poetry and science, and what we may mean by it. Bearing Wordsworth in mind, we will move on now to the next difficulty, that of the pathetic fallacy, and look at a work which, brief though it is, forms in this respect an interesting complement to some of Dr. Needham's thought here: *Rediscovering Natural Law* by Scott Buchanan.[6]

This is an enquiry into the concept of natural law as it affects science and jurisprudence, deploring the long-standing split between them. Like *Science and Civilisation in China* which also discusses this subject (Vol. II, Section 18), this work belongs among many efforts nowadays to reunite what has unluckily been separated in past intellectual history; yet it too exhibits at times a certain negativeness towards other dynasties. Its particular value for us here, however, is that it champions that form of the human metaphor which may, negatively, find itself dubbed pathetic fallacy; and does so explicitly in the name of reason.

The purpose of this small work is to claim a fresh right of speculative freedom for jurisprudence in its theory and methods. The right is claimed, however, by extension for other disciplines as well.

The way of speculation is now, as always, beset with threatening presences, on one side, religious dogma, and, on the other, empirical science. The effect so far is timidity in speculation. A part, the essential part, of natural law doctrine, is speculative in both senses of that troubled word. It must be theoretical in its insistence in dealing with the facts for what they can yield in the way of knowledge, and it must dare to go beyond facts, to explore and exhaust what the always meagre data indicate in the way of abstract knowledge. This is to say that we must recognize, trust, and follow reason, wherever it leads . . . In one sense there has never been a time when reason was more cultivated and trusted than it is now, but this is true only when reason gives

[6] Published by the Center for the Study of Democratic Institutions, Santa Barbara, California (Fund for the Republic, Inc.), 1962. I am indebted to Mr. Joseph Morello for drawing my attention to it.

itself to mathematics and when mathematics renounces any claim
to truth. Most of the other uses and levels of reason are suspect.

(p. 32)

It is not entirely clear what the writer means by religious dogma
in this context, nor by mathematics renouncing claims to truth, but
the main gist is clear enough. He is at work upon this word "reason," he too fearing lest it be shrunk into a formalist and dogmatic
orthodoxy.

Adopting in the main the terms of Aristotle, and identifying
"reason" by means of them, he claims that, in our modern practice
and even more in our modern attitude, we have eliminated from
the vital workings of speculation two essential faculties of the
mind, the first the "so-called discursive understanding" which is
"the reasoning from one hypothesis to another or from hypothesis
to principles," the second, "intellectual intuition, the power by
which the mind first seizes and contemplates an intellectual object."
To this latter capacity, which with Aristotle or Aquinas he calls
a habit of mind and which he distinguishes from "hunches and emotional ecstasies, although these may contain insights needing clari-
fication," he ascribes the power of the still-unexplained primary
induction, in science or elsewhere.

He proceeds then to give an illustration of the kind of freedom
in speculation which he means; and the kind of thought chosen by
way of demonstration proves to be that use of the human metaphor
we have been considering. Mr. Buchanan deals, in this connection,
with the epithet of "pathetic fallacy":

We are shocked, romantically moved, or amused when we read
Virgil's demonstration of natural love as the pivotal insight
around which the *Divine Comedy* moves; when we read of the
loves of the magnets in Gilbert; when Kepler attaches "intelligence" to the orbits of the planets; or when Francis Bacon or
Leibniz allows events to perceive one another. We allow the
latter-day theologian to warn us off these modes of thought by
telling us that these are only poetic analogies inspired by far-
off divine events. Or we allow the devotees of "scientific method"

to tell us that such events are vestiges of primitive animism and superstition. Actually these poetic and scientific makers of the modern intellectual world were thinking in a bold and highly rational style about ends and means. They were not indulging in what we call pathetic fallacies, the imputation of psychic powers to inanimate things. It is we who are prisoners of the pathetic fallacy; we substitute occult powers for legitimate objects of rational processes.   (p. 34)

Here too there is a recognition that modern thought may be shifting from a rigid univocal dogmatic method to others, including the use of the human metaphor so clearly exhibited in the examples quoted. The writer adds, immediately after the last passage, that this is "a late and tentative revival of the full rationality."

Once again it is reason that is appealed to, as the basis of the working of the human metaphor. We will carry this forward with us as we turn to look at the last of the three difficulties which may obstruct our understanding of that method's workings: certain modern approaches to the subject of psychology.

IV

In his *Treatise on Method* of 1818 (Section II, Head 16), Coleridge introduces, with an apology, the term "psychology." The context has its significance. Not only does he adduce, as in the parallel passage in *The Friend,* the greatest poet of all as an instance of working to a Method, or *the* Method, but he adds this: "Shakespeare was pursuing two Methods at once; and besides the Psychological Method, he had also to attend to the Poetical." Against the word "Psychological" an asterisk directs us to a footnote: "We beg pardon for the use of this *insolens verbum;* but it is one of which our language stands in great need. We have no single term to express the Philosophy of the Human Mind . . ."

There is a psychology, as well as a method, among the poets. In Coleridge and Wordsworth, the two poets who have accompanied us in this Chapter as masters in the matching of outer and inner universes, it reaches a high degree of development both in theory and practice. It connects very closely with the human metaphor itself.

Here, once again, we may face a difficulty. The term "psychology" is likely to call up in our minds the great developments in this branch of study some eighty years after Coleridge's tentative turning to the word. So widely disseminated among us have the premisses and methods of this later movement become that we are liable to accept them nowadays, even in the often imprecise form in which they reach us, as self-evident. We assume that this is what psychology means and is. Yet here too, in layman and professional alike, that "liberal open-mindedness" as against "formalized orthodoxy" is needful if we are to appreciate the poets' proceedings.

Their essential difference lies, it seems to me, in the appeal which the poets make to Reason, both as the directive of the method and the key to the psyche. We have already marked this appeal in Wordsworth's *Prelude*—only one of many in that work, particularly in the summing-up in Book XIV—and have used it as a negative clue, to eliminate two interpretations of the method and metaphor which are inappropriate. It will serve now as a positive clue, for the better understanding of the methods employed in this psychology and the view of the mind which it is grounded in.

Reason: you may have noticed in that methodological passage we quoted from Wordsworth something not far off a paradox. The poet simultaneously turns to reason and away from scientific method as such. Specifically it is analysis which is rejected as an instrument for investigating psychological subject matter: who shall parcel out his intellect; hard task to analyse a soul; and so on. The contrast with much modern psychology, exhibited in the very term "psychoanalysis" and the preoccupation of many in this discipline with attaining or maintaining scientific status for it, is plain, and needs no comment. Our question takes a slightly different form: is Reason something other, or something more, than scientific method? We have just been looking at someone other than a poet, Scott Buchanan, who says yes to this. The poets say yes too. What they wish to develop and to add in are the synthetic powers of the reason as well as its analytic ones. The exploration and development of forms of thought of this kind is part of the total work of poets in regard to Method in general, and there is reason to believe that it is going to be increasingly important in the present age which with its considerable analytic powers is all lopsided.

In Wordsworth's methodological statement in *The Prelude* which we have been considering, this turning to synthesis takes the form of refusing to attempt to divide up an indivisible subject. Another form of it, to be seen in practice in that poem, and set out in theory by Coleridge in *The Friend* and *Aids to Reflection,* is a refusal to split off observer from observed.

We are accustomed, or rather conditioned, to regarding the separation of observer and observed as one of the necessary requirements for what we call objectivity. In this we are already perhaps a little out-of-date, for in certain respects this formal exclusion of the observer, as a rigorous requirement in scientific method, is already on the way out among scientists themselves. The methodological question confronts psychology particularly plainly, for it seems unavoidable that in normal, as distinct from abnormal, psychology, the working intellect has got to investigate itself. The inclusion of the self may then be merely recognition of this fact. Wordsworth recognizes this in his research, or poem, and offers his own mind as subject matter. Coleridge, when he approaches the question, defines reason ultimately as self-affirmation, and its work as "the contemplation of reason, namely, that intuition of things which arises when we possess ourselves as one with the whole, which is substantial knowledge, and that which presents itself when . . . we think of ourselves as separated beings, and place nature in antithesis to the mind, as object to subject, thing to thought, death to life. This is abstract knowledge, or the science of the mere understanding" (*The Friend,* Section II, Essay XI). The contrast between reason and science, in these terms, comes out clearly.

We can see how such an approach would justify the human metaphor as a method adapted to synthetic operation of this sort. Before we return to that, however, we need to be clear about the self which is being included in the method. Poetic psychology differs from the modern psychological or psychoanalytic movement in two ways here. First, it is primarily interested in the normal mind and body, and in their functions of thought and imagination. Second, it starts out from a different view of the human organism.

The contemporary psychological outlook postulates, as is familiar to us all, an unconscious within the organism and personality, together with a collective unconscious. This is, by definition, something of which the conscious part of us is not aware but by which we are powerfully influenced. Both Coleridge and Wordsworth are aware of an unconscious. Coleridge uses such a concept in connection with Shakespeare when lecturing on him, and one might equate with it that "undersoul" of which Wordsworth speaks. The basic principle of the poets' psychology, however, is not division but unity. It postulates an integrity in the entire human organism, not as a desideratum but as a fact, with a hierarchy of various powers and activities which are yet held together in the central purposiveness and selfhood which characterize any living thing, and man most of all. Of this organic unity, the directive and bond is Reason. We have to cast out of our minds any dry remnants of eighteenth-century dust that may cling round that word. This is the Reason which is, above all, self-affirmation. It is one with the living faculty of Imagination, as Wordsworth says when he finally characterizes that mysterious and marvellous power, in Book XIV of *The Prelude,* as "Reason in her most exalted mood." Where distinctions are made between one faculty and another, the emphasis in this psychology is always on reuniting. Within this integrity of the whole, the various bodily and mental powers of the human organism, such as perception, feeling, emotion, imagination, intelligence, love, appear as levels, in each of which the over-all and all-embracing activity—call it thought, reason, or being-human—is carried on. Coleridge says in this connection in an extraordinary sentence in *Biographia Literaria,* Chapter XII, "For sensation itself is but vision nascent, not the cause of intelligence, but intelligence itself revealed as an earlier power in the process of self-construction." (It was from here that I took the phrase of "self-construction" as a description of mind and man at the very beginning of this book.) The idea that thought or reason or intelligence is diffused over the whole human frame is a marvellous and a modern one,[7] but it is not yet very familiar to us, and that is why we need to pay attention to it, since the psychological attitudes in which we are raised tend to be rather different.

There is one final such difference to be noted, between the poetic approach and that of contemporary psychology, before we return to the human metaphor itself. We shall misunderstand what is going on in the poetic method if we regard its figures as "symbols," whether sexual or archetypal, proceeding from the unconscious of the individual or the race. Of course we think with all of our bodies including our sexual powers, and share with our congeners in history the great figures which creation offers us; but the rivers, stars, vegetation, mountains, winds, which are wedded in this operation to human qualities and events, are not "symbols" standing for this or that. The notion is as foreign to poetic method as a code would be. The images of natural phenomena and the mental, emotional or bodily states or happenings that partner them are not symbols but figures or crossing-points in a complex and flexible net of relations which the mind establishes or perceives between the two universes, inner and outer, for the purpose of interpreting each, in one of the basic operations of human method and thought.

We can return now to the human metaphor itself. Since it is a long time since we looked at it directly, we will take a fresh example. This is a letter of Coleridge's, dated 1820, to an unknown correspondent, left unfinished without conclusion or signature. It is valuable here because it begins with exposition and goes on to example. (It is also the best help to the understanding of The Ancient Mariner that I know.)

[7] Cf. Michael Polanyi's argument, in Personal Knowledge, in favour of admitting the presence of a "tacit component" in all knowing and thinking, part of that "peripheral awareness" which is a factor in every such situation and which complements the "focal awareness" of directed attention and skill. This tacit component cannot be formulated and is in its inarticulateness akin to and continuous with bodily skills. It is an integral part of all knowing and thinking.

For from my very childhood I have been accustomed to *abstract*
and as it were unrealize whatever of more than common interest
my eyes dwelt on; and then by a sort of transference and transmission of my consciousness to identify myself with the Object
—and I have often thought, within the last five or six years, that
if ever I should feel once again the genial warmth and stir of
the poetic impulse, and referred to my own experiences, I should
venture on a yet stranger and wilder Allegory than of yore—
that I should *allegorize* myself, as a rock with its summit just
raised above the surf.ace of some Bay or Strait in the Arctic Sea
"while yet the stern and solitary Night Brook'd no alternate
Sway"—all around me fixed and firm methought as my own
Substance, and near me lofty Masses, that might have seemed
to "hold the moon and stars in fee," and often in such wild play
with meteoric lights, or with the Shine from above which they
made rebound in sparkles or disband in off-shoots and splinters
and iridescent needle-shafts of keenest Glitter, that it was a
pride and a place of healing to lie, as in an Apostle's Shadow,
within the Eclipse and deep substance-seeming Gloom of "these
dread Ambassadors from Earth to Heaven, Great Hierarchs"
and tho' obscured yet to think myself obscured by consubstan-
tial Forms, based in the same Foundation as my own. I grieved
not to serve them—yea, lovingly and with gladsomeness I abased
myself in their presence: for they are, my Brothers, I said, and
the Mastery is their's by right of elder birth and by right of the
mightier strivings of the hidden Fire that uplifteth them above
me—

It is not, I think, fanciful to see in this astonishing passage Coleridge's final comment upon his own nature, his failure and achievement, the loneliness, the paralysis of the will, the nature of genius,
the poetic tradition, the relation of these two to grace, seen as they
can only be seen in a figure or metaphor (or allegory in the poet's
own words, a form of the human metaphor we shall be coming to
shortly). It has both beauty and terror in it, for the ice which earlier
had been no more than caves supporting a pleasure dome, or from
which even a guilty voyager could be delivered, has got him at
last in an Arctic of no return. Yet what a splendour in this miraculous mindscape, even though, as he cries out so movingly, the

greater splendour is not for him! Using it as an example of method
in the human metaphor, when inner and outer universes are related
to one another, we can draw certain conclusions from it.

First, this is a distancing manoeuvre or technique, necessary if
the self is to investigate the self, or normal mind to investigate
normal mind; the abnormal mind is already somewhat distanced by
its abnormality. The mind can observe itself-and-not-itself under
the figures it has chosen to embody itself in. A choice of forms
adequate to the purpose, and the contemplation of those forms
now in a dynamic fusion with the mind or self, enable humans to
perceive the nature of their own mental operations, not directly
but clothed in figure and thus made visible, and to engender mental power for further advance in this way. There is nothing out-
landish about this. It is how most if not all thought works, and
anyone familiar with the queer effort of thinking will recognize it,
even if it presents itself to us often in seemingly more abstract
forms. It is akin to the process Coleridge describes in one of his
Notebooks: "thinking" is letting the mind construct its figures and
watching the mind construct its figures. Thus Michael Polanyi in
Personal Knowledge (Part II, Chapter V) describes the mathematician thinking: "He works his way towards discovery by shifting
his confidence from intuition to computation and back again from
computation to intuition, while never releasing his hold on either
of the two." Both suggest a balance, simultaneous yet sustained
by alternating shifts of attention, between the construction of figures and the contemplation of the self's activity with them, in
some unexplained yet vital unity.

From such a technique, two things seem to follow. First, all
thought on any subject can also be an occasion for thought about
the mind, and possibly should be. If the mind when it figures can
always contemplate itself under those figures, the scope and op-
portunities for self-contemplation and interpretation are very great.
Secondly, there is a suggestion that perhaps mind is best investi-
gated in this way.

There may be a further reason for the adoption of this figuring
technique in investigating the mind. If we look at Coleridge's example of it, we cannot fail to be struck by the very wide range

of implicit imaginative and bodily responses it calls into action: the ice, eternal solidity offset against meteor-flashes, heights and depths, eight different forms of light-reflections and refractions exactly specified, and so on. It is possible that this is a way of calling up an adequately complex yet orchestrated instrument, bodily, imaginative, intellectual, to deal with so complex a subject as any mind must be, let alone this one. This notion is suggested, it seems to me, in a passage that occurs in the last book of *The Prelude*. Like the earlier passage from that poem which we looked at, it is once again methodological:

> Then might we return
> And in the Rivers and the Groves behold
> Another face, and hear them from all sides
> Calling upon the more instructed mind
> To link their images with subtle skill
> Sometimes, and by elaborate research
> With forms and definite appearances
> Of human life, presenting them sometimes
> To the involuntary sympathy
> Of our internal being, satisfied
> And soothed with a conception of delight
> Where meditation cannot come, which thought
> Could never heighten.

The passage is interesting for its mention of subtle skill, synthesis of images, and elaborate research (you may remember we said that Wordworth was going to use that word in connection with what he was doing in this poem). Yet it suggests something more, by that "sometimes" one thing, "sometimes" another. It suggests a double method at work, a calling in of more than one level of operation in the human organism. This figuring which is part of the human metaphor and the poetic psychology and method may enlist the co-operation not only of those top levels of reason which we term intellect—Wordsworth here calls them thought and meditation—but also of those less articulate and more bodily levels of operation, which, as he says here and elsewhere, and as Coleridge would bear him out, take their Reason so to speak under the form of delight or joy. As anyone knows who has thought or imagined, the co-operation of these other levels, in any task which is to be vital and not just conventional, is as essential as it is unaccountable. Such factors in thinking may be merely obscured in this context if thought of as unconscious. To figure the mind in terms of perceived, visual, auditory, tactile images may help to call them into action. The full powers of the human organism are needed if it is to fulfil its interpretative work and itself fill out the organic half of the human metaphor.

That brings us, briefly, to the last point I want to draw from Coleridge's sustained metaphor of his mind. It is not just an image of him as he was at one moment of time. The whole of his life history is there, either implicitly or explicitly, and were we to take the other related images in his earlier poems we should find something not unlike the work Wordsworth was attempting in *The Prelude,* where not merely the present of the organism but its past and future, its life-story in fact, is to be used as part of the human metaphor in its (now allegorical) operation. This will be the subject of our last two Chapters.

Four

INDIVIDUAL LIFE AS MYTH: THE FIGURE OF SUFFERING AND EFFORT

I

SO FAR WE HAVE BEEN CONSIDERING USES OF THE MIND-BODY figure as an interpretative instrument in the great range of forms or figures which constitute the universe, and, conversely, how those external figures may interpret happenings in the body-mind. The next stage of our enquiry admits of a new dimension, that of time. We shall consider now the possibility that this mutual figuring process need not be limited to moments or instantaneities, but may extend over periods of time. That is to say, if the living dynamic of an organism may be an instrument for thinking with, so may the narrative history of that organism.

Every organism has a life history, but only in the most complex and remarkable organism of all, man, does the life, in part at least, control and direct its own history with consciousness, again in part at least, of what is going on. (This incidentally creates a problem for scientists like Dr. Needham who now propose an organismic approach to nature; is the human organism with these strange inherent elements of consciousness and responsibility to be the paradigm, or some arbitrarily selected organism lower down the ladder?) It is the human metaphor, however, that we are concerned

114

with, and what we now confront is the possibility that the individual human life, seen in its totality in so far as that is possible, may in its turn form one term of a metaphor and be an instrument, therefore, for divining or interpreting something beyond itself.

This entails a number of changes in our framework. First, on more technical gounds, we must bear in mind when we think of metaphor itself not merely the classic form of it, X is Y, but such forms as allegory where the figure entails not only entities but also a story. Next, the considerable expansion of one term of our metaphor, comprising now the human life with its full complement of body, mind, heart, spirit, experience, presupposes a similar expansion of the field which this metaphor, of which human life is the X (we do not yet know what the Y may be), may be used to explore. The postulation of a new field of operation becomes unavoidable as soon as we move forward to take account of man in his full stature of consciousness and moral responsibility. Such a field cannot be bounded by what we understand in general by the phrase "the natural world," particularly as delimited at present by official scientific thinking. We have to postulate, clearly and deliberately, and then attempt to understand, a further level of operation. The theory of emergence in evolution with its concepts of levels each embracing the full properties of less highly developed levels but advancing beyond them into new frames of reference would offer some such outline for the extension of our thought. The human life, if used as a metaphor or instrument of interpretation, is not going to tell us about lower levels of organization. It is going to tell us about itself, and something beyond itself.

Another change in our method, consequent upon this, is that we turn for help at this point to dynasties other than that of the scientists. The enquiry in this stage is not wholly reducible to the nature which they have so faithfully pursued, in company with the poets and with us, thus far, and their discipline in its present terms cannot encompass the X of our metaphor now, human life in its full meaning. Scientists as such (but please be reminded that it is perfectly possible to dwell in two or more dynasties at once, given the power and the inclination, to be scientist and philosopher, say, or scientist and priest and so on) have, as they themselves constantly remind us, neither instruments nor credentials for this kind of research. In considering then the possibility of employing the figure of the human life as part of an interpretative instrument for further understanding, to which dynasties in particular can we turn?

The answer seems to be that this extension of field, out of (but not utterly separate from) nature into the field in which man as conscious being operates, involves four and a half of the seven dynasties. The half, I suggest, are the musicians from among the practitioners of the non-linguistic arts; we shall not be stopping with them but it does seem that their art, besides being a web of pure and complex relations in time is also capable of being, as George Bernard Shaw admirably says in one of his notes as a music critic (in the *Pall Mall Gazette,* 31 October, 1887), "answers to unspoken questions of the heart . . . ghostly echoes from another world." We shall not be stopping either with the next dynasty, that of the historians, though we should certainly remember them as fellow-workers here, for present and future reference. Once past these, we come to the three dynasties which are more closely concerned with setting up the problem of human life as metaphor and attempting to explore it. They are the philosophers, the poets and the priests.

The first indication we shall look at comes from someone who falls rather between the first two of these three dynasties, Thomas Mann. In a lecture which he gave in 1936, subsequently published among his essays, he says outright, "One may as well say 'lived myth' as 'lived life'." Here is a clear preliminary "X is Y": the individual human life is myth.

We need to be quite clear that this is a metaphor, not a proposition or a statement of identity. Strictly, a life is not a myth. A myth is some traditional story, imagined or based on actual events, often closely connected with a rite, whose tenor gives the mind the sense that it is capable of revealing more than just itself. Hence the longevity of myth, its frequent correlation with religion, and its use by the poets as an instrument of thought. Ultimately a myth is entirely the product of human making. A human life is not. "The individual human life is myth" is a metaphor, therefore, but we need to see also that it is a metaphor, or figure of thought, which includes a figure of thought as one of its terms. When we originally spoke of metaphor and looked at the range of figuring thought which includes it, myth was one of the forms of that thought.

We are going to find a number of other comparisons between human life and some form of artifice of the figuring mind. For the present, however, we will glance at Mann's ideas in this essay, which are valuable in their own right.

The subject of Mann's essay is Sigmund Freud. He called it *Freud and the Future*,[1] but says at the end that a better title might have been "Freud and the Myth." Throughout, Mann considers Freud as an investigator, conscious or unconscious, of this metaphor, "Human life is myth." Freud is one of the people we shall consider in Chapter V, so we shall not stay with him now. Perhaps, however, I should say that when I mentioned earlier that we were taking leave of the scientists at this point, I had Freud in mind, for we are not taking leave of him, and the little syllogism I am implying holds good. Despite Freud's own anxious carefulness and the yet greater anxiety of some of his followers to keep within the bounds of a rather narrowly conceived scientific method, he is often better understood in terms of other dynasties' disciplines, and it need not surprise us that Mann in examining Freud turns to a philosopher, who proves to be capital for us, not merely because he states clearly the problem of "apparent design in the fate of the individual" which is the title of one of his works, but also because he proves so fertile in varieties of the metaphor, "Life is a myth," which Mann proposes. This philosopher is Schopenhauer. The work of his to which Mann directs us is *Transcendente Spekulation über die anscheinende Absichtlichkeit im Schicksal des Einzelnen*, of 1851. Mann calls this essay "a marvel of profundity and penetration," and he shall introduce us to it.

He first summarizes Schopenhauer's drift as follows:

The pregnant and mysterious idea there developed by Schopenhauer is briefly this: that precisely as in a dream it is our own

[1] *Essays*. Translated by H. T. Lowe-Porter. Vintage Books, New York, 1957.

will that unconsciously appears as inexorable objective destiny, everything in it proceeding out of ourselves and each of us being the secret theatre-manager of our own dreams, so also in reality the great dream that a single essence, the will itself, dreams with us all, our fate, may be the product of our inmost selves, of our wills, and we are actually ourselves bringing about what seems to be happening to us (p. 312).

These two first metaphors for human life, life as a dream, life as drama, and the connectedness of them, are central to Schopenhauer's thought, both of them wonderful "third aspects" for divination but beyond the scope of this present book. Notice that both dream and drama in their respective fashions are human products, artifices of figuring thought. Mann emphasizes the drama metaphor and expands it into some wide notion of artifact which shall include ritual and religious mystery:

His character is a mythical role which the actor, just emerged from the depth to the light, plays in the illusion that it is his own and unique, that he, as it were, has invented it all himself . . . Life in the myth . . . is a kind of celebration . . . it becomes a religious act . . . it becomes a feast . . . In antiquity each feast was essentially a dramatic performance, a mask; it was the scenic reproduction, with priests as actors, of stories about the gods . . . The Christian Middle Ages had their mystery play . . . The artist eye has a mythical slant upon life, which makes it look like a farce, like a theatrical performance of a prescribed feast, like a Punch and Judy epic . . . It only lacks that this mythical slant pass over and become subjective in the performers themselves, become a festival and mythical consciousness of part and play (pp. 317 ff.).

The idea of the process being partly conscious is important, and he reiterates it:

Let us suppose that the mythical point of view could become subjective; that it could pass over into the active ego and become conscious there, proudly and darkly yet joyously, of its recurrence and its typicality . . . One might say that such a phenomenon alone could be the 'lived myth'; nor should we think that it

is anything novel or unknown . . . It was a mythical identification, peculiarly familiar to antiquity; but it is operative far into
modern times, and at all times is psychically possible (pp.
318 ff.).

It is good that consciousness of living life as myth should be suggested as part of the validation of this metaphor, since consciousness is one of the determining characteristics of human life itself.
It seems to follow also from Mann's remarks that, if life can be
interpreted in terms of myth, the latter in its turn may be interpretable only when fused with the human life, in a situation of
formal, even solemn, reliving such as drama and religious ritual
make possible. These are useful insights, and we may have cause
to remember them later on. Now we will proceed, as Mann directs
us, to Schopenhauer, and may have a surprise; for where we
thought to find a philosopher we come upon somebody much more
like a poet.

Schopenhauer carries his thought forward throughout this essay
by means of metaphors. Mann has already introduced us to two of
these, and we shall find many more. This procedure is not an aberration on our thinker's part; it is deliberate: "It is given us to grasp
the deepest and most hidden truth no otherwise than in image
and likeness," he says in this very work. He calls his essay a Speculation, insisting that it is not the answer to, but the statement of, a
problem, and he speculates by means of figures. I am giving the
substance of his thought below, for his language falls, as German
philosophy is liable to do, into very long complicated sentences,
and paraphrase works better here than direct quotation.

He begins by examining the particular feature of human life
to which shortly he will suggest a number of metaphorical analogies. His starting-point is the belief, held by certain people, that
the apparent necessity which shapes their lives is not merely a
blind force of chance; that it can be looked at as purposive, and
that that purpose is discernible by the individual concerned, sometimes only in flashes, sometimes over a complete life-span. Such
a belief may induce the conviction that the life of the individual,
no matter how much of a muddle it appears, is in reality a shaped

and ordered whole. The work of shaping the life is carried out by three factors, and the individual life is the product, not just the result, of their interaction: first, our instinctive drives which constitute our own inner necessity: second, our fully conscious and reasoned actions: and, third, the falling out of external circumstance and chance. These three may so "play into one another's hands"— *sich wechselseitig dergestalt in die Hände arbeiten*—that they leave an impression, when all is completed, of a well-rounded and perfected work of art, even though while the process was going on it was usually impossible to make out any design or direction in it. If we conceive of such a process at all, we may do so in terms, the philosopher says, of "a secret and inexplicable power" guiding our lives, often against our inclinations or our best judgment, in the interests of an over-all pattern we may or may not perceive. Because of the uncertainty in our minds about this, we regard the particular tools of this power—accidents, so-called, or errors on our part—as interruptions or flaws in the life pattern. Yet this is itself an error, for the apparent total accident is only, Schopenhauer here maintains, a necessity which has come to us by a more roundabout route. He uses that very image, "ein auf entfernterem Wege hergekommenes Nothwendiges." "The significance of this as a whole," he concludes at the end of the first half of the essay, "would depend on whether the subject were a rather commonplace individual or someone out of the ordinary."

Schopenhauer next searches for some means of identifying this designing power operating in human lives. He notes earlier identifications—Fate, daimon, genius, Providence. All these are for him "imaging and allegorical conceptions of the matter in hand." In his search he leaves behind him classical myth and the Christian religion, and turns to science. Could the concept of Nature, considered as the drive towards form and order in the universe at large and as "the inner purposiveness which reveals itself unambiguously in the single organism," be identified with the force which appears to shape human lives? Before this can be answered the question arises, for Schopenhauer as for other thinkers we have been concerned with: What is the nature of Nature? Significantly in view of what we already know about the battle of metaphors at this point,

Schopenhauer has recourse at once to metaphor and image as the means of tackling the question. He wants a metaphor for Nature which will match its dynamic and purposive force and so perhaps serve as metaphor in turn for that apparent mysterious force in human lives. He tries out a number of images to this end.

The first, and most elementary, is that of mechanism—"mere mechanism" as Schopenhauer says. Above this and controlling it —Schopenhauer's thought is teleological throughout—is something he calls the *Technik* of Nature. To translate this one might need the Greek *techne,* or technique, or even technology, with its implications of human and social organization beyond any level of "mere mechanism," a figure very close to Carlyle's thought, and employed explicitly by Marx in *Das Kapital.*[2] This over-all field of force or work once grasped, Schopenhauer goes on to suggest that it cannot be understood through what has become the accepted figure for interpreting cause and effect, the figure of the chain—the "causal chain" still so familiar in our speech and thought. Instead, he says, we must try to envisage the individual chains or series as a net,[3] "a

[2] "Darwin has interested us in the history of Nature's Technology, i.e., in the formation of the organs of plants and animals, which organs serve as instruments of production for sustaining life." *Capital,* tr. Moore and Aveling, London, 1938, Vol. I, Ch. XV, p. 367, fn.

[3] This shift, from "chain" to "net" as working metaphor is, it seems, part of the general shift of figure going on in Western thought and science. Vico in the *Scienza Nuova* is already rejecting, as a basis for his thinking about history, not merely the familiar "blind concourse of atoms" but also, in his own phrase, the "deaf chain of causes and effects," his metaphor pointing up a lack of necessary organic qualities in such figures. In 1803 the phrase, "the kindling net," is used in Erasmus Darwin's poem, *The Temple of Nature,* to express the spread of organic life over the globe. Carlyle, in his essay "On History," 1830, says, "Alas for our 'chains,' or chainlets, of 'causes and effects,' which we so assiduously track through certain handbreadths of years and square miles, when the whole is a broad, deep Immensity, and each atom is 'chained' and complected with all!" Once again it is Dr. Needham, in Vol. II of *Science and Civilisation in China* (see particularly Section 13, pp. 280 ff.) who draws attention to what is happening in the figurative thinking of Western science, and the contribution that can be made by the characteristic thought-patterns of Chinese science: "A number of modern students . . . have named the kind of thinking with which we have here to

vast, all-embracing, multiply-interwoven net, which likewise moves forward with its whole expanse in the direction of time, and which in fact constitutes the temporal universe."

In the end he reverts to his own great myth, that of the vast inexorable impersonal *Wille* which drives that complex net, the universe, and all within it, including human lives. Confronted by the problem how blind necessity can yet, in the individual life, produce the appearance of over-all design and significance, he does not make a direct answer but again approaches the question through a series of metaphors, taken this time not from Nature but Art. The figures he chooses are: the individual human life as art form, as set of didactic figures, and as epic poem. (Here, too, occur

---

do, 'coordinative thinking' or 'associative thinking.' This intuitive-associative system has its own causality and its own logic. It is not either superstition or primitive superstition [sic] but a characteristic thought-form of its own. . . . In coordinative thinking, conceptions are not subsumed under one another, but placed side by side in a *pattern*, and things influence one another not by acts of mechanical causation but by a kind of 'inductance' . . . The key-word in Chinese thought is *Order*, and above all *Pattern* (and if I may whisper it for the first time, *Organism*) . . . Things . . . were thus parts in existential dependence upon the whole world-organism. And they reacted upon one another not so much by mechanical impulsion or causation as by a kind of mysterious resonance" (Pp. 280-81. Italics in the original). After connecting this type of thinking, in differing ways, with Blake, Lévy-Bruhl, and Whitehead whom he considers the supreme example of it in the West so far, and after introducing the great metaphor for this moving pattern of relations, Dr. Needham sums up in one sentence: "In such a system causality is reticular and hierarchically fluctuating, not particulate and singly catenarian." Out of which coruscation of Latinity let us extricate our metaphors, for *reticulum* is a net and *catena* a chain. That the net, now become a key figure, is to be thought of in terms of organic and not mechanical structure is brought out a little later: "The characteristic Chinese concept of causality in the world of Nature was something like that which the comparative physiologist has to form when he studies the nerve-net of coelenterates, or what has been called the 'endocrine orchestra' of mammals . . . it is now becoming probable that the higher nervous centres of mammals and man himself constitute a kind of reticular continuum or 'nerve-net' much more flexible in nature than the traditional conceptions of telephone wires and exchanges visualised" (p. 289).

the linked metaphors of life as drama and dream.) As ways of thinking about possible design in the individual life, he turns not merely to art but, more specifically, to poetry.

If poetry is in some way to figure the hypothetical shaping element in human lives, we might expect the poets themselves to be aware of this and concerned in it. So in fact they are, and they corroborate Schopenhauer's selection and use of these three figures. Take the first, for instance, life as art-form. Here is Carlyle, in *Sartor Resartus*, "Of this latter sort are all true Works of Art: in them (if thou know a Work of Art from a Daub of Artifice) wilt thou discern Eternity looking through Time; the Godlike rendered visible . . . But nobler than all in this kind are the Lives of heroic god-inspired Men: for what other Work of Art is so divine?" The poets, however, do not affirm these variants of the metaphor merely in speech or in theory. They see their own lives in this way, as shaped into an art form, a series of figures, a poem. In other words, for poets and by extension for some of those who write about poets,[4] the activity of poetry is not merely the model by which the "apparent design in the fate of the individual" might be interpreted; poets are themselves examples of that class of beings Schopenhauer refers to, who believe that their own individual lives show such a shaping force, a significant design. Poets both employ the metaphor, and see their own lives as instances of it at work.

If we take the second form of Schopenhauer's metaphor, life as a set of figures "harmonious and of didactic intent" as his phrase runs, we can see both aspects of the poets' approach in something Goethe says. He uses the metaphor, but what is more, uses it about himself. He is answering a question about where he got the idea for his play *Torquato Tasso*. "*Idea?*" he snorts—you can hear the snort in Eckermann's account (May 26th, 1827)—"I had Tasso's life, I had my own life, and in the process of combining two such mar-

---

[4] Cf. for example, Leslie Fiedler, *Love and Death in the American Novel*, New York, 1960, p. 409, "Like Poe himself, Griswold approached his subject's [Poe's] life as if it were a work of art. So also did Baudelaire . . ." Or George Steiner, *The Death of Tragedy*, London, 1962, p. 172, "Goethe's disposal of his manifold energies was his greatest work of art."

vellous figures with their idiosyncrasies the image of the *Tasso*
rose up in my mind." Goethe uses the word *Figur* for his life, and
for Tasso's; both poets, we may recall. The fusion of the two life-
figures which he suggests is interesting too, connecting with our
surmise earlier that a myth can only be grasped fully when it is
fused with a life being lived, in just this way.

The work of art, which was Schopenhauer's first and general
metaphor for some process of shaping and design in the individual
human life, takes now a more specific form. With the second stage
of the metaphor, the set of figures, we encounter the series, the
narrative. This comparison will interest anyone who has ever tried
to manage a prolonged imaginative narrative—a novel for instance;
for there does seem to emerge from the work itself some kind of
guiding instinct such as may appear in certain lives also, directing
and warning off, of which one is not fully conscious or, to put it
exactly, which one carefully avoids looking at but commits oneself to while the work is in progress, and whose congruence and
foresight can amaze one afterwards. (There is a connection here,
I believe, between this sense of direction and fittingness and those
inarticulate Rules of Rightness which Michael Polanyi in *Personal
Knowledge* postulates for any skilled activity.) After narrative fiction, or rather inevitably accompanying it as I believe, come allegory and myth, corresponding yet more closely to this second
metaphor of Schopenhauer's—life as a set of didactic figures. Beyond these again, but closely connected with them all is the third
stage of his metaphor: life-as-poem,[5] whether epic or dramatic.

It is this form of the metaphor, the individual life as allegory or
as poem, that we are now going to consider. Two poets provide
the evidence. The first is Keats, writing, in a letter of 1819, "A Man's
life of any worth is a continual allegory." The second is Milton who

[5] The beautiful phrase of "life-become-poem" is applied to Goethe
by Albert Schweitzer in "Goethe's Message for our Time" (1932), included in *Goethe,* London, 1949: "That the great author by this service
as an official and in his labours dedicated to Science stands before us
as the man who knows neither Great nor Small, but does all that he
does with conscientiousness and devotion, is so arresting a life-become-
poem that it could not be outweighed by any other poem he might have
given us in its place" (p. 48).

says in *An Apology for a Pamphlet*, 1642, "And long it was not after, when I was confirmed in this opinion, that he who would not be frustrate of his hope to write well hereafter in laudable things, ought himself to be a true Poem." Again the poets vindicate the philosopher's figures, but again also they do more than this—they offer themselves into the figure, so to speak. Keats does not specifically relate his statement to his own life; one does not claim to be a man of worth in those terms. He is speaking, however, as we shall see in a moment, in a context of poets and poets' lives, and the example he gives is Shakespeare, the poet with whom he so passionately identified himself. If Keats did not already hold his life to be allegory, he must have wished that it one day might be. Milton, in his turn, is speaking in this pamphlet about his own life. We have then to see what their poetry and their lives can tell us about human life as poem, allegory, myth, metaphor, that is to say, when it takes on a significance, a power of divination, beyond itself.

The passage in Keats's marvellous poem-studded letter, or journal, which he was writing from February to April of 1819 to his brother and sister-in-law in America, and from which we have drawn so far just the one sentence, runs as follows:

> A Man's life of any worth is a continual allegory—and very few eyes can see the Mystery of his life—a life like the scriptures, figurative—which such people can no more make out than they can the hebrew Bible. Lord Byron cuts a figure—but he is not figurative—Shakespeare led a life of Allegory; his works are the comments on it.

We find ourselves full in the company of the poets at once. Not all poets lead figurative or mythic lives, it seems, but some do. The figuring in such a life is related (Keats indicates this twice over) to the figures which operate in religion, and this indication is the more interesting since Keats was not a believing Christian in any precise sense. Further, where a poet lives such a life, his works will comment upon what is going on in that living figure or myth, implying at least some degree of consciousness of what is going on

in the poet concerned. Whether the comment is for the poet's own
benefit, for that of a possible audience, or both, is not made clear.
The wording of Keats's statement suggests that the life of the poet
may be his primary art-form, his works being secondary to that.

A life as an allegory, i.e., an art-form taking the form of figures
akin to the figures in religion,[6] a poet as an instance of this, his
poetical works providing the commentary on the allegorical life—
this is what Keats proposes for us to consider.

Such a proposal departs widely from current practice in literary
criticism. Indeed, if the poet's life is the allegory, or, as Milton says,
the poem, and the written poems are the commentary upon this,
as Keats says, then criticism as we know it recedes into some uncertain third place, becoming comment on comment, gloss upon
gloss. In addition to this divergence, the prevailing school of criticism today makes an absolute separation between life and works
in a poet or writer, and directs its and our attention exclusively to
the works. There have been good reasons for this, but obviously
we shall need here some method less exclusively literary. Such a
thing is nothing unheard-of in the critical tradition. The critic of
genius who comes at once to mind is Sainte-Beuve, who seems to
have been reaching himself towards considering life-and-works in
the writer as a hypothetical organic whole operating in an ecological
field and shaped by some such force as Schopenhauer was feeling
after, and who says outright that his discipline is analogous to that
of the natural scientist.

Commenting on one's own life, as Keats says the poet does, may
sound unpleasantly self-conscious; yet in fact the process, known
as a reality by all poets of a particular kind, the strange dialogue
between poet and work in which the former asks from the latter
illumination on the mystery of his life, is scarcely conscious while
it is going on at the time of writing, becomes clearer only later, and
would be vitiated at once by any posturing introspection or self-
dramatization. I think it is on these grounds that Keats rules out

[6] An interesting comment on this insight of Keats, relating it to the
close connection between the "historical" and the "symbolical" in individual lives and to modern psychological thinking, occurs in Owen Bar-
field's *Saving the Appearances*, London, 1957, p. 151.

Byron as an example of the process. A certain distance is achieved by the poet working not as biographical critic or as self-historian, but in terms of figure.

This rules out autobiography direct as part of the process. When poets take up autobiography their essential energy is not running in its main channels. Even the most obvious precedents seem to support this, for Wordsworth turned to autobiography, as he explains to Coleridge in the beginning of *The Prelude*, in order deliberately to evade what he felt to be a "block" in his productive capacity, while Goethe's autobiography, *Dichtung und Wahrheit*, is far less instructive about his life than his imaginative works are, and he is a particularly pertinent example because he is the kind of poet who figures himself in everything he writes, including, incidentally, the scientific work. The inadmissibility of autobiography here is implied by Keats in that methodological statement of his already quoted, for the example he gives, of allegorical life and commenting works, is Shakespeare, of whom we possess not one scrap of direct autobiographical statement apart from a hint or two in the Sonnets. Yet "his works are the comments," that is, his dramas, themselves figurative works. Comments on life-as-figure take the form of figure in their turn. Only through myth, apparently, can the mythic potential of the individual human life be revealed.

From what Keats says, presumably any work produced by such a poet would be relevant as commentary, but on grounds of comprehensiveness I am choosing a late work in each case; that is to say, the work of a man of 63 and a boy of 24. Milton's is a tragedy, *Samson Agonists*, 1671, Keats's a narrative poem, the second version of *Hyperion*, sometimes called *Hyperion: A Vision*, sometimes *The Fall of Hyperion: A Dream*, 1819.

The two poets choose the figures for their comments from different sources, and their choice directs our attention to the field such figures can be drawn from. There seem to be five main sources of narrative at the poet's disposal: history public or private, legend, myth, religion, and narratives newly invented by the poet himself. Although the last class sounds as if it were of a different kind, it has a strong tendency to merge with or at least to reflect figures from the four traditional sources. We can see this in *The Fall of Hyperion* itself. A personal narrative invented and told in the first person in form of a dream, it yet connects at once with the Garden of Eden, then merges into traditional Greek myth. Milton chooses a Biblical story from the Old Testament, which his title, his preface, and his whole approach tie up with classical Greece. Each, it may be seen, is deeply traditional, suggesting that a life-figure, at this its point of transfiguration which is also its exegesis, calls on the support of, or reveals its place in, the living tradition of past and future to which it belongs. The mysterious illumination which in broad daylight the three dearest disciples suddenly saw around the figure of their Master and the apparition of Moses and Elias conversing with him, that episode which Christians call the Transfiguration, comes to mind here.

To take up one of the traditional figures of mankind is to take up, since the story is already "a tale that is told," a fixed form. As with all fixed forms, it requires great power and discipline in the artist to keep it intact yet revivified. It means rejecting, on the surface, all facile experimentalism or innovation or even overt originality for the sake of the resources such a form may disclose out of itself. Milton comes near to meeting this challenge almost perfectly in *Samson Agonistes*. In his Hyperion poem, Keats, so much younger and very ready to learn, does not. His struggles at this point are illuminating for the whole transfiguring process at this stage, and it is with the younger poet, therefore, that we shall begin. (I would point out that there is an excellent commentary on the relation between Keats's life and works in John Middleton Murry's *Keats and Shakespeare;* Chapter XII deals with *The Fall of Hyperion.*)

Keats wrote two versions of this his last poem of any length, the second, with which we are concerned, providing a long dream-preface to his original tale. In the first he relates the story of the struggle between the dispossessed titans and the sky-god Olympians. He sees undoubtedly that these are master-figures for operations and powers within the mind. Gods are one of the best methods of divining what is going on within, a great instrument of psychological research, as Vico saw, Freud surmised, Nietzsche vindicated in *The Birth of Tragedy*. Yet Keats cannot be held within this frame. In the third and last Book of his earlier *Hyperion* he breaks out, in part at least, in his reworking of the figure of the Olympian god, Apollo. This god is by tradition the god of music and poetry; what Keats confronts us with is a young and as yet only half-formed god, dimly aware as an adolescent, albeit a divine one, might be of some great calling that is his, but uncertain what to do with the lyre he has dreamed of and then woken to find beside him, and asking, as Apollo does in the poem "Where is power?" To him at this point there appears the majestic female form of Mnemosyne, who in Greek is Memory and the mother of the Muses. Her power of vision, which he somehow catches, infuses into him the power of poetry and of genius which is to fulfil in him his true nature and calling. The transformation, however, is—in the twenty-four extraordinary lines which conclude the apparently unconcluded poem—terrifying,

> Most like the struggle at the gate of death;
> Or liker still to one who should take leave
> Of pale immortal death, and with a pang
> As hot as death's is chill, with fierce convulse
> Die into life: so young Apollo anguished.

The full power of poetry, so this figure says, is the task of a god, yet demands a total and agonizing transformation of that god's being. This was Keats's preliminary comment on his life.

It is interesting that we find in Milton a similar preliminary figuring, not of a god but of a godlike hero, Orpheus, the embodiment and image of the poetic vocation, and as the myth has it and Milton reminds us, torn to pieces by the profane only to transcend death in some mysterious inextinguishability of the poetic genius. As early as *Lycidas,* Milton identifies the poetic calling with this tragic myth, but in general rather than in particular; later, in that interesting autobiographical passage at the beginning of Book VII of *Paradise Lost,* he draws the connection plainly between this figure and his own life. Yet even so it is not his final word, any more than the first Hyperion is that of Keats.

The difference between the early and the later Hyperion is two-fold. The first we have already noticed—the introduction of dream and of the dreamer-narrator. The second has to do with form. The first Hyperion is a narrative poem with heroic and mythological content. The second Hyperion before it merges with the narrative of the first is much closer to dramatic form, falling roughly into a prologue and three acts. Each act ends with a kind of death, but since this is a dream, the protagonist is resurrected to continue the action, repeated a second and third time. We know that Keats intended to write plays had he lived longer, but now it is as if he were groping towards some combination of narrative and dramatic form to express what he wants to say, his comment upon his life.

The scene, leaving aside the prologue for later consideration, opens in a green and mossy arbour, embowered in leaves and blossoms. You will recognize it if you remember Keats's *Ode to Psyche* from the last Chapter, "the wreathed trellis of a working brain"; in other words we are inside the mind, looking at it. You may ask: where else but inside the mind can one be in a dream? True; but you may have noticed, too, when theatre-going, how often stage sets give one this same sense—that they present something within one's own head. The stage here is empty. Someone has been there recently, but has gone, leaving the remnants of a giant meal, fruits which the dreamer eats, and a cup of cool transparent juice. This the dreamer takes in his hands,

> And pledging all the mortals of the world,
> And all the dead whose names are on our lips,
> Drank. That full draught is parent of my theme.

This is an extraordinary toast: all the now living, named by that name which says they are going to die, and all those already dead who yet live in our memory of their worth. Something may be expected to happen after this; and indeed it does, and rapidly. The innocent-looking draught for which the poet thirsted produces an effect more sudden and overpowering than any opiate, philtre or poison; all three are mentioned and rejected as comparisons. None, the poet says,

> Could so have rapt unwilling life away.
> Among the fragrant husks and berries crush'd
> Upon the grass, I struggled hard against
> The domineering potion, but in vain.
> The cloudy swoon came on, and down I sank . . .

This is the first death of the play, and the end of Act 1. The death is painful, not in itself but because the victim battles with it. Instead of succumbing quietly, as he might well have done, he struggles; even this first death, then, is a contest, an "agon" in the Greek phrase for ritual contests between athletes or contending poets. This is a lonelier fray.

He comes to himself to find everything changed. The garden is gone. In its place is a colossal half-ruined temple, closed up towards the east, while to the west stands one titanic image, an altar and a distant figure, a priestess, ministering. He approaches the altar steps. Now comes the second crisis of the story, for the voice from the altar tells him that his life is forfeit if he does not climb up the sacred steps before the dry leaves she already holds over the sacrificial flame are consumed away. How true to dream or near-nightmare this is:

> the tyranny
> Of that fierce threat and the hard task proposed,
> Prodigious seem'd the toil; the leaves were yet
> Burning, when suddenly a palsied chill
> Struck from the paved level up my limbs,
> And was ascending quick to put cold grasp
> Upon those streams that pulse beside the throat.
> I shriek'd, and the sharp anguish of my shriek
> Stung my own ears: I strove hard to escape
> The numbness, strove to gain the lowest step . . .
> One minute before death, my iced foot touch'd
> The lowest stair; and, as it touch'd life seem'd
> To pour in at the toes; I mounted up . . .

Here is a second death, even more abrupt and unexplained than the first, much more intense and full of fear, for this time it is a clear challenge thrown down by some power outside the self. Perhaps the drink was too, but this time it is unmistakable and pitiless.

The third death follows soon. It accompanies the poet's admission, which he prayed for and was granted, to the visions which move behind the priestess' face, "bright-blanch'd" in some intolerable effulgence of death and pain and love. We see now that she, Moneta, is one with the Mnemosyne of the earlier narrative, but the dreamer is very far from being the god Apollo. His humanity, with its inherent humiliation, is what is laid before us:

> Without stay or prop
> But my own weak mortality, I bore
> The load of that eternal quietude . . .
> And every day by day methought I grew
> More gaunt and ghostly. Oftentimes I pray'd
> Intense, that death would take me from the vale
> And all its burdens; gasping with despair
> Of change, hour after hour I cursed myself . . .

The third death makes yet more plain the form and meaning of the first two. Struggle is once again the core of the pain, a struggle which, however, is neither defiance nor pride at meeting overwhelming challenge. It is only weakly, miserably, humanly, that the sufferer endures; yet endure he does. To this third death, or prolonged life-in-death, there is no resurrection. The narrative continues, wearily, with the old tale already told in the first version of the poem, and after a little while breaks off with a note, in the printed versions, 'Here MS. ends.' One remembers the last line of Keats's prologue, "When this warm scribe, my hand, is in the grave." Even the preamble to this poem ends with a death, the real death which waited for this boy within two years and which, as we can see from the context, is mentioned not with any intent of self-pity but as part of the assaying process which forms the action of this drama. The nature of this is growing clearer, illuminated particularly by the description of the third and last death. The struggle at the center is a superhuman effort to correspond, in the theological sense of the word, with a vocation.

What vocation, what activity? The poem itself asks this question, and the clearest hints towards an answer seem to be given only at the crises of suffering, *in articulo mortis* as it were. The first death moves the dreamer out of one dream into another, more powerful and more numinous. The second brings him up to the altar and into converse with the more-than-mortal servant of the gods. The third, before which he utters the wonderful and fearful prayer, "Purge off . . . if so it please thee, my mind's film," takes him into the vision of the gods themselves. Listen to that last passing-over:

> there grew
> A power within me of enormous ken
> To see as a god sees, and take the depth
> Of things as nimbly as the outward eye
> Can size and shape pervade . . . I sat myself
> Upon an eagle's watch, that I might see,
> And seeing ne'er forget.

Seeing—what intense concentration on that activity there is in these lines! Sight, the power of seeing, insight as in the above passage, vision, dream—these are the activity, the central purpose which the poem is about.

It would be easy, and up to a point true, to argue that seeing in this sense, which is also remarking, grasping, interpreting, is the essential calling of the poet, the 'seer.' Yet if this were all, Keats could have rested content with his first Hyperion as the comment on his life's figure, the young poet-god in his solitary task. It is very significant that he was not content. The enquiry which a poet pursues in life and works is not a technical one, for poets only. Some wider human aim is implied already in the reworking of the vision. In the second poem we are concerned with something beyond any professional concern of the poet as such.

This is made explicit from the very beginning of *The Fall of Hyperion*. The prologue discusses one of the forms of the essential vocation of vision the poem deals with, the nature of dream. Keats says, first, that fanatics dream and create by their dreams "a paradise for a sect." The savage dreams but his dreams, lacking the preserving power of great poetic tradition, are lost. "Poesy alone can tell her dreams," Keats says, and thus can rescue imagination from dumb oblivion. It looks like professionalism after all, but then he continues,

> Who alive can say
> "Thou art no poet—mayst not tell thy dreams?"
> Since every man whose soul is not a clod
> Hath visions and would speak, if he had loved,
> And been well nurtured in his mother tongue.

This needs careful reading. Only poets can tell their dreams, but no one can forbid any man to tell his dreams on the grounds that he is not a poet. That is, Everyman *is* a poet; once again a great poet is saying, as Goethe does, as Wordsworth does, that poetry is no charismatic speciality but every man's birthright. Now we understand the difference between the fanatic, who with his dreams caters only to an élite, religious or aesthetic, and the poet. The crucial question is raised by the prologue's final lines:

> Whether the dream now purposed to rehearse
> Be poet's or fanatic's will be known
> When this warm scribe, my hand, is in the grave.

The matter is taken further in the conversation between dreamer-poet-narrator and priestess in the temple. Humanity is seen here as consisting of three groups. First, there are ordinary people, content and at home in the world as it is, neither seeing nor feeling the anguish abroad in it. Such, the priestess says, should they ever enter the temple (which is already, you remember, vision within vision) cannot surmount the challenge to climb the holy stair, and "rot on the pavement where thou rottedst half"; she reminds the poet that he is not so very different from them after all. Only those are admitted here, she adds,

> to whom the miseries of the world
> Are misery and will not let them rest.

This admits the dreamer-poet, as the narrator's living witness shows and as Moneta further explains; but it also admits another group beyond the second group of poets, and it is about the third group that the dreamer asks. He speaks to her of the thousands who, loving their fellows unto death, share the common agony of the world and labour to help and assuage it. He is puzzled: why is he here alone and not they? He asks, in fact, about the saints.

We have already an interesting trio—everyman, poet-dreamer, saint, the middle group related each way yet distinct. The poet may have a little more power of vision and suffering than everyman, but everyman is an essential in what is going on. The differentiation between poet and saint is expressly stated by Moneta herself:

> "Those whom thou spakest of are no visionaries,"
> Rejoin'd that voice; "they are no dreamers weak . . .
> They come not here, they have no thought to come;
> And thou art here, for thou art less than they . . ."

The saints' power of vision and suffering is transmuted into the active loving life of charity and good works, and the poetic visionary vocation is declared to be absolutely subordinate to it. The judgment here is clear and right but it will be misunderstood if it is thought to be a belittling of the poetic function. The very struggle of the dreamer in the poem to fulfil his vocation belies any such thing. This is not derision but diagnosis: the weakness appears as a concomitant, even a necessary condition, of what is going on.

A scheme is beginning now to take shape. Keats's poem presents the poet, in relation to everyman and saint, as a human being full of weakness yet passionately committed to a central energy of purpose, that of vision and more vision. Increase in visionary power is won through a series of ordeals, each of which is an encounter, conscious and agonizing, with some form of death. Such is the formalization one can draw up for *The Fall of Hyperion,* imparted, as we remarked earlier, in a form which merges narrative with drama.

Perhaps already this may seem to you suddenly familiar. Narrative of an all-embracing quest, struggle through a series of deadly ordeals, the frequent sadness of impending death, Gilgamesh, Achilles, Roland—this is a large part of Western epic poetry. And again, vision which is purchased, through mortal weakness, at the cost of irremediable loss and pain: put it that way, and the mind at once answers "Tragedy" and calls up Oedipus, King Lear, and Milton's own Samson who awaits our attention shortly. If we have followed Keats at all rightly, his poem-comment has brought us to epic and tragedy, if only in a fragmentary form, where Milton, in the longer life and full powers granted to him, will bring out the full flower of each.

Lest we should now imagine that we have landed up in the safe and insulated haven of literary technicalities, it is very important that we should call to mind at once two things. First, the process or method inherent in this work of Keats does not relate to poetry or to epic or tragedy. It relates to life, real, lived, suffering, desperately hard to understand. Keats says the works are the comment on the life as allegory. Second, this is for poets true of all their work. Living poetry does not have anything to do with literature, a fact more and more disguised from us by the impressive mausoleum which literary studies in modern education have erected around it. Poetic forms like epic and tragedy are still what they always were, systematic instruments by which to interpret life. From this working point of view, which is also ours, epic and tragedy are not defined sub-branches of literary categories, neither are they dead, as critics are all too ready to maintain (as well speak of the death of logarithms) though one remembers also, gratefully, the countering voices, Rachel Levy setting T. E. Lawrence in the epic tradition in her enquiry into epic literature, *The Sword from the Rock*, London, 1953, or the approach of the Russian poet, Ivanov, to *Dostoevsky and the Tragic Life*, published in translation in New York, 1957. They are specialized methods developed for and by the poetic dynasty in the task which it shares with certain others of its compeers, the enquiry into significance in human life.

III

Epic and tragedy are, in Western culture, very near relatives. They rank together with certain other of our great Forms, in mathematics, music, religion and perhaps philosophy, among the major contributions to the advance of human thought. Tragedy is of the West alone. Epic we share with other cultures, but differ from them in that Western epic from the beginning leaned towards tragedy. The Epic of Gilgamesh, a modern commentator tells us—N. K. Sandars in *The Epic of Gilgamesh*, Penguin Books, Harmondsworth, England, 1960,—"is a mixture of pure adventure, of morality, and of tragedy," and the central figure is "the first tragic hero of whom anything is known." "The *Iliad* is the primer of tragic art," says George Steiner in *The Death of Tragedy*. We began, apparently, as we meant to go on.

We may know, historically speaking, that epic and tragedy are close kin, but we tend to let them fall apart in our minds. Only if we reconnect them shall we see that Keats, in reaching towards both, was not overreaching himself but simply working within the tradition of his dynasty. In Milton's time the tradition was still clear on this point; Cleanth Brooks in his introduction to Milton's works in the Modern Library College edition, New York, 1950, reminds us that "Milton, like other writers in his time, counted epic and tragedies as twin varieties of the heroic poem." We find the poet commending the two in double harness, "Heroic Poems, and Attic Tragedies," in his treatise of Education, 1644. In his foreword to *Paradise Lost* he calls that epic a Heroic Poem, just as he calls his tragedy, *Samson Agonistes*, a Dramatic Poem. The mingling of the two in his work is as clear as in that of Keats.

This tradition of unity is still open to us, poetically speaking, and we are going from now on to avail ourselves of it, abandoning any absolute division between epic and tragedy and employing instead the notion of the heroic poem as a single instrument.

In Western culture, tragedy was to be so important that it infused itself into epic from the start. Western heroic poetry tends to have a tragic cast. The reasons for developments and continuities of this kind within a culture are hard to come at, but we may assume that forms such as these take root, flourish and persist because they are germane and vital to what are and will be the central preoccupations of a civilization, having the same kind of prophetic interpretative power possessed by other formal instruments such as good metaphors or hypotheses. No one culture can pursue all, or even many, of the great questions presented by the universe to its latest comer, man. It suffices, as in individual lives, that each choose some few for particular research.

From the start, the shape of Western heroic poetry seems to make clear that we chose, or more precisely our poets chose for us, together with our priests, a vast enquiry into the nature and meaning of human action united with suffering and death. The extraordinary hypothesis put forward and tried out in heroic poetry, which like all hypotheses declares its interpretative powers only gradually, generation by generation, is that human suffering and death, in a context of particular struggle, are instruments of learning and discovery. The West adores to learn, to know. St. Paul and Aquinas set their Heaven here—"Then shall I know even as also I am known"; "These three run together: vision, the perfect knowledge of an intelligible end; comprehension, the presence of that end; delight or enjoyment, the ease of lover with beloved."

Suffering, weakness, death are not, in themselves, tragic; this is common knowledge. If, however, to these shared pains of all humanity there is brought a particular kind of active effort, so the poets glimpse, which is neither convulsive nor defiant, those occasions can become knots or agons where something can be learned. (The notion of effort as essential to the learning process is upheld by what we know so far of its psychology.) This learning is to be thought of as communal, as well as individual. The heroic and tragic struggle is not a knot in a single chain, to revert to Schopenhauer's and Dr. Needham's figure for a moment; it is a knot in a wide net. Hence the audience presupposed by tragedy, and perhaps by epic too.

This is the instrument heroic poetry has forged for itself. We should keep it in mind as we turn now to Milton's use of it. We shall find in his poem, as in that of Keats, the vocation to one energetic purpose, pursuit of true vision, advance by ordeal, and suffering and weakness seen not as impositions but as essential elements in the functioning of the process of life and learning. It is good in a way to be going backwards in time like this, from nineteenth to seventeenth century, for it may prevent us from ascribing the similarity between Milton's and Keats's work simply to "literary influences." The elder poet was indeed one of the most loved (and because most loved, most threatening) ancestors of the younger one, but what we need to see is the broad tradition which embraces both of them and to which each, in his own time, contributes.

Milton chooses as the figure for his life-as-poem the traditional Biblical story of Samson, the ancient Jewish hero of the early struggles with the hostile tribe of Philistines, a struggle at once political and religious, and makes of this what he calls a dramatic poem. Even as the Bible tells it this is a strange story: the angel-announced birth of a child who is to deliver Israel from the Philistine yoke, the heaven-sent gift of phenomenal strength by which great deeds are performed on the enemy at overwhelming odds, the hero who is a maker of riddles and a crafty answerer of leading questions but not quite crafty enough where woman is concerned, for part of the story is of Samson's pursuit of first one, then a second, then a third Philistine woman, against his parents' remonstrances, and the last betrays him when he at length confides to her the secret of his superhuman strength—that it resides in his uncut hair. She waits till he sleeps, has his hair shorn off, and then delivers him to his foes, who put out his eyes and take him to their capital to slave for them in menial work and to be a gazing-stock for national pride. Yet in the end Samson triumphs, although at the cost of his own life. Brought out publicly to make sport for the Philistine assembly by his feats of strength, he grapples the central supports of the building housing them all and brings it down in ruin upon their heads and his own.

For the action of his continuous five-act drama, beautifully shaped in the classical manner, Milton takes the last twenty-four hours of Samson's course. The play is set in Gaza, the Philistine citadel; yet its action is also, as in Keats's dream, within the mind, for its author says in his foreword that it was never intended for the stage. In Milton's handling of this subject, Samson, first seen in abjection under his terrible fate and in bitter self-reproach, is condoled with by the chorus of fellow-Israelites, visited and admonished by his old father Manoa, then by his wife Dalila, to whose blandishments and final threats he is unrelenting; he next outfaces the braggart bluff of the Philistine giant Harapha, and lastly is summoned by a public officer to his enemies' assembly, from whence comes first the terrible outcry and next the report of his final deed of destruction and triumph, whereupon the play closes with a marvellous elegiac celebration of courage and loss.

The centres of anguish in the play, as the opening makes clear, are three: blindness, slavery—which two connect: "Blind among enemies, o worse than chains"—and impotence, again related to both the above and imaged in Samson's loss of physical strength, yet only imaged for the real weakness was within: "O impotence of mind in body strong." The prime weakness is that of the man with the divine mission of power who could not keep its holy secret "but weakly to a woman must reveal it." So, too, the actual blindness and captivity are also only images of their counterparts inwardly, born of that same central weakness, his servitude to a woman, "True slavery, and that blindness worse than this."

In this poem too, as in Keats's, the central figure must undergo a succession of ordeals, to be faced in the blind humiliation of self-knowledge and in helplessness. The formal symmetry of the Miltonic with the Biblical narrative is remarkable. Samson has in the past been required to face a triple testing, while still in his full strength, and failed. Three times he has refused his wife, Dalila, the secret she asked; the fourth time he succumbed. In the play this is answered by his facing three ordeals, and then in the last triumphing. First he meets his old father who in the tenderness and pain of their situation yet confronts his son with the real nature of what he has done: betrayed not just himself but Israel's God for the sake of woman. Idolatry begets idolatry, for Manoa relates how in Samson's fall is exalted Dagon, the idol deity of Philistia: "This, Samson, of all thy sufferings think the heaviest." The next encounter is with woman herself, and as we might expect, in terms of mortal combat. After Dalila withdraws, repudiated but defiant, the third ordeal comes in the person of the Philistine giant, Harapha, to taunt Samson, the former warrior, with his blindness, filth and helplessness, while yet keeping well out of his reach. This scene is highly formalized, given its shape by a thrice-repeated challenge, on Samson's part, to single combat, not as man to man which could be prompted by pride, but as champion to champion, Jehovah against Dagon, which challenge the Philistine refuses. So the action proceeds to the last deed of all, Samson's summoning to the Philistian assembly and that return of strength by which he is enabled to annihilate the flower of his God's enemies, at the price of his own death.

The point—the puncturing point of the action—is the weakness itself. This cannot be too strongly emphasized. In this play it takes the form, within a human being, of divinity and erotic love tangled in a blind knot. It is one of our constantly recurring themes: the Tiresias who is physically blind yet the seer confronting a King blind in all but the physical sense and living in sexual horror, in *Oedipus Rex;* the pronunciation upon Gloucester's adultery in *King Lear,* "That dark and vicious place where thee he got/ Cost him his eyes." Who sees, who is blind? The question is put before us over and over again, with the price for not seeing; it is there again in St. John's Gospel, that account of unremitting agon between Messiah and His hostile people, after the healing of the man blind from birth: "And Jesus said: For judgment I am come into this world; that they who see not may see; and they who see may become blind. And some of the Pharisees who were with him, heard: and they said unto him: Are we also blind? Jesus said to them: If you were blind, you should not have sin: but now you say: We see. Your sin remaineth."

It is this weakness, typified by blindness, which is at the heart of the play in every sense; for when we come to the central Act III between former husband and wife we find that what they struggle over is the nature of weakness and strength, the latter called by its older name of "vertue" which connects with both courage and power. Dalila first pleads feminine weakness as the cause of her betrayal of her husband; then she taunts him with male weakness in being beguiled by her out of his secret, and says

of the pair of them, "Let weakness then with weakness come to
parl." Samson has to admit the justice of her accusation, but refuses the excuse of weakness for his own action: "All wickedness
is weakness." Dalila ends by a total reversal of her position. Suddenly she claims for herself not weakness but virtue on grounds
of piety to her country, seeing herself now a national heroine, and
so departs while Chorus meditate on virtue and marriage in terms
of love and battle. It seems the final revelation of Samson's inner
blindness, the misery and venom of the object he had loved too
well.

This is the crisis of the tragedy and its turning-point, for the
weakness which entailed helplessness and blindness is also the
point of revelation. Samson by the time Milton's play begins has
already suffered the classic *peripeteia*, the fall from great fortune.
He speaks of it himself in Act II, brooding on his former glory:

> All mortals I excell'd, and great in hopes
> With youthful courage and magnanimous thoughts
> Of birth from Heav'n foretold and high exploits,
> Full of divine instinct, after some proof
> Of acts indeed heroic . . .

There is the key word, entering quietly. It is not taken up again
during the main body of the play. Only after the final catastrophe
will it return. A great paradox is at work here, for at the point of
crisis the tragic reversal is itself reversed. Only in blindness is the
final revelation possible. The seeming contradiction is brought out
in one of the last choruses, whose subject is Samson's death: the
Philistines are spoken of as "with blindness internal struck," while
Samson

> though blind of sight,
> Despis'd and thought extinguisht quite,
> With inward eyes illuminated
> His fierie virtue rouz'd . . .

and the combination, of true vision and of virtue, is carried forward
through the surge of the remaining lines, with metaphor on meta-

phor, dragon first, eagle next, and finally the great sole Phoenix rising from the flames of death and destruction, "then vigorous most/ When most inactive deem'd." Immediately after the phoenix chorus, the cry and the key word are taken up by Manoa, with the repetitive stamp of final authority:

> Samson hath quit himself
> Like Samson, and heroicly hath finish'd
> A life Heroic . . .

The nature of heroism or heroic virtue is what Milton's poem is about, but *Samson Agonistes* is only the end of a lifetime of living heuristic into this, through the instrument of the heroic poem. (I think possibly Corneille's production of tragedies tended the same way.) Heroic poetry is no mere technical term.

Milton's research into this question comes out most clearly, perhaps, in the opening of Book IX of *Paradise Lost*. He pauses there to consider both his instrument and his quest, the nature of heroic poetry and the nature of heroism. The passage is central not just to our pursuit here but to the whole poem, for this is *its* turning-point. The Fall of Man approaches, the first sin of the first man in the Biblical story, and the epic poet says, "I now must change/ Those notes to Tragic." His hero, Adam, will fall from primal perfection into the weakness, misery and mortality humans must endure for ever after, and Milton chooses this moment to assert heroism at this point and in these terms[7]—weakness, suffering, death—and to discuss too the role of epic in this evolution of heroism, as ideal and as living reality. In lines 13-41 of this Book the word "Heroic" is repeated no less than five times.

We begin with a challenge. Sad argument, the poet says, yet "not less but more Heroic" than that of the *Iliad*, the *Odyssey*, the *Aeneid*, all of which he refers to in the next few lines. Heroism, and epic, in a poet's mind, evolve. He reaffirms his own choice,

---

[7] It was their failure to grasp the nature of Milton's work on heroism at this point, its revelation in weakness not in strength, which misled Blake and Shelley into thinking Satan, not Adam, was the real hero of *Paradise Lost*.

"this Subject for Heroic Song / Pleas'd me," his subject being man, not gods or demi-gods or even obvious heroes, "hitherto the only Argument / Heroic deem'd"—man in his weakness. He dismisses military prowess as beside the point, and is even more cavalier with the outward trapping of chivalry—"Not that which justly gives Heroic name / To person or to Poem." The order and juxtaposition of those last two nouns seem interesting. After all these negatives he puts forward his own concept of heroism: "The better fortitude / Of Patience and Heroic Martyrdom . . ." If patience seem as drab to us as virtue tends to do now, let us remember that in every Latin-born language it declares its descent, along with "passion," from *patior:* I suffer. Strength in weakness, suffering, apparent defeat, death—Keats's pattern holds up well. It will figure Milton's thought yet further.

Adam, the epic and tragic hero of *Paradise Lost,* is Everyman. He is the hero in weakness, as Samson is; but there is a third figure here, and this figure corresponds to Keats's third member of the trio, the saint. This third figure Milton calls, in one of his youthful poems, "Most perfect *Hero*" and he will develop this insight all through his working life. In Christian theology this figure has come to be called the Second Adam. It is one of the names under which Jesus Christ is named, and Milton calls Him hero in his unfinished poem, *The Passion.* This hero will not depart from the pattern of heroism Milton has put forward; He suffers, is subject to weakness, meets death and apparent defeat, and is, through this and not in spite of it, the hero *par excellence* in this poet's epic and tragic questioning. There is an extraordinary consistency in poetic thought. Already in that early poem Milton adds to his phrase "Most perfect Hero" the adjunct, "tried in heaviest plight / Of labours huge and hard, too hard for human wight." The progress and trial by ordeals are already present. After Milton has finished with the heroism of the first Adam he will return to that of the second in *Paradise Regained,* the short Biblical epic published in the same year as *Samson Agonistes,* and immensely relevant to it. It recounts the three temptations of Christ in the wilderness, three clear ordeals once again, endured and surmounted faithfully but in weakness, not strength; this is the heroism. Book I of *Paradise Regained* is

essential if we are to understand what Milton was after. Already
in lines 15-16 he is speaking of "deeds / Above heroic, though in
secret done." Almighty God, recounting His purposes, makes clear
once again the nature of the hero:

> But first I mean
> To exercise him in the Wilderness,
> There he shall first lay down the rudiments
> Of his great warfare, ere I send him forth
> To conquer Sin and Death, the two grand foes,
> By Humiliation and strong Sufferance:
> His weakness shall orecome Satanic strength . . .

We see next the Son of God musing upon His destiny and on possible "heroic acts" in older and fiercer terms, only to reject them
and to see, some fifty lines later

> This chiefly, that my way must lie
> Through many a hard assay ev'n to the death . . .

The significant pattern built up by Western heroic poetry once
again receives here signal and detailed confirmation.

It receives this confirmation, and expansion, I must point out,
not in Milton's mind but in the person of Christ Himself and in His
life story. This was from the beginning the centre and scandal of
Christian belief, and there is comment on it, in a wide human
context, already in St. Paul, "And he [the Lord] said to me: My
grace is sufficient for thee: for power is made perfect in infirmity
. . . For which cause I please myself in my infirmities, in persecu-
tions, in distresses, for Christ. For when I am weak, then am I
powerful." In Christ the figure of heroic virtue (that phrase applied
still in the Catholic Church officially to canonized saints) under-
goes a metamorphosis which is at the same time a fulfilment of the
insights of the prophetic and poetic tradition of the Jews and those
of seers elsewhere in the West.

Such an approach, by working poets, to matters of religion and
particularly to Christianity may give rise to two difficulties. The

first is literary or methodological. It seems to be very generally held that the relationship between tragedy and Christianity is understood once and for all, namely, that they are mutually exclusive. I can only say that working poets do not see things in this way, the nature of tragedy being for them a living changing instrument for the extension of human understanding, and Christianity a storehouse of treasure which may be applied to the poetic quest. This leads into the second difficulty, that such a connection may appear sacrilegious. Keats's and Milton's careful distinction of levels of operation as between poet and saint is to be remembered here, but this difficulty turns also on the modern tendency to isolate religion from the other heuristic endeavours of man, whether in underestimation of its value or a desire to keep it duly protected. Such isolation, whether for negative or positive motives, reduces religion to irrelevance. No poet at work on the central needs of human understanding in the heroic tradition can accept such a separation of his own from the other great dynasty specifically and hieratically concerned with the question of the significance of human life. Indeed the two poets we have been working with draw the connection very closely.

Keats in his poem related the dreamer-poet to everyman and saint. Milton explores the nature of action and suffering in everyman and Holy One in *Paradise Lost* and *Paradise Regained;* but their exploration is not merely in the poetry. We may remind ourselves now that we took the two poems, *The Fall of Hyperion* and *Samson Agonistes,* both of which turn out to be heroic poems, as, in Keats's phrase, comments on the life-allegory or life-poem of the poet concerned. "A life like the scriptures, figurative" Keats says. It is the life ultimately, not the work only, that is to conform to the pattern we have seen so far. We come, therefore, to the two lives as heroic poems.

IV

Milton's life, taken from any point of view, is a remarkable one. Running from 1608 to 1674, it spans that vital and struggling century when England cast off absolute monarchy with violence, experimented with a theocratic commonwealth, and rejected that in turn for a constitutional monarchy under which modern institutions, political and economic, would be free to develop and presumably to put aside that monarchy also when it should be seen to be of no further service. Milton appears in these stirring times in one guise after another; the young academic at Cambridge, laying the foundation of his immense scholarship, no meek clerk but a fighter already, rejecting publicly the narrow philosophy his conventional university offered him, and refusing to become a minister in the Church of England because it seemed to him servitude; the deliberate withdrawal into private life to cultivate himself for his task of poetry, by studies, the classics, music; the cultured traveller in Europe, addressing learned societies in Italy, visiting Galileo in prison, speaking his mind, not always discreetly, about the Church of Rome, who gave up the dearest pilgrimage of any classicist, the voyage to Greece, to return home at the news of impending civil war, there to throw in his lot with the Parliamentary forces; the political and theological polemist, attacking authority and set forms in church government and liturgy, campaigning in favour of divorce, upholding freedom of the press against censorship, whether political or ecclesiastical; appointed by Cromwell Secretary for Foreign Tongues to the Council of State, becoming thereby an active member of a successful revolutionary government whose action in beheading the former king he consistently defended; then, after the demise of that government and the restoration of the monarchy, the proscribed and then reprieved rebel; last, the elderly man in enforced retirement who returns to poetry and produces his last great works. This is the outline. There are two exceedingly important notes to be added: the blindness which overtook him in middle life, and the passionate nature which ran to three marriages and continual thought, in the prose and the poetry, on the nature of woman and of the relation between woman and man.

The centres of anguish and struggle which Milton figures in Samson are the blindness and the deliverance to political enemies, on which he had commented jointly in one of the personal passages in *Paradise Lost*, Book VII,

> On evil days though fall'n, and evil tongues,
> In darkness and with dangers compast round,
> And solitude

and the vulnerability which comes through a strongly erotic nature. That Samson is Milton in figure is not hard to see; what is more important is that we realize that the operation going on in Samson is hinted at as paralleled in the poet also. In Milton's earlier and very well-known sonnet on his blindness, after he has made his complaint he is answered by Patience. Anyone who sees this as merely self-admonition to resignation will miss the mark completely. This is the very turning-point itself, of weakness to virtue in heroic terms. The self-same word is at the heart of his epic, "the better fortitude / Of Patience and Heroic Martyrdom," and of his tragedy, for just before the woman enters there is a great chorus on this matter, "Extolling Patience as the truest fortitude." It is applied to Samson, but there are notes later in the chorus which bring Milton rather than the Israelite here to mind, where former strength is seen as relegated in the dark ways of God

> . . . to th'unjust tribunals, under change of times,
> And condemnation of th'ungrateful multitude.
> If these they scape, perhaps in poverty
> With sickness and disease thou bowst them down,
> Painful diseases and deformed,
> In crude old age.

We who see Milton now in the light of his subsequent fame must make the effort to see the end of his life as it must have appeared to himself. Shelley caught it in that moment when he says, in *Adonais,*

> Lament anew, Urania!— He died,
> Who was the sire of an immortal strain,
> Blind, old, and lonely, when his country's pride,
> The priest, the slave and the liberticide,

Trampled and mocked with many a loathed rite
Of lust and blood: he went, unterrified,
Into the gulf of death . . .

It is a double insight that made Shelley seize so clearly the note
of death and apparent defeat, the note of tragedy, in fact, at the
close of Milton's life, and also made him include, on these terms,
Keats among the immortal strain of descent stemming from the
earlier heroic poet. For *Adonais* is "An Elegy on the Death of John
Keats, Author of ENDYMION, HYPERION, etc."

Keats was born in 1795 and died in 1821. This too was a period
when much was happening in England and in Europe, but Keats
was not *engagé* in public life in the way that Milton was. He was
the eldest of a family orphaned as children, and the close bond
of affection between them (in this they are like the Wordsworths)
and the sense of responsibility which Keats himself bore towards
his sister and brothers come out in the wonderful letters which
he wrote all his life and which we are lucky to have had preserved
to us. After some schooling he spent a year or two on the fringes
of the medical profession; then, always in straits for money and
up against the legal guardian of the family, took the decision to
devote himself entirely to writing poetry. His first major work was
met, on its publication, by some of the most savage criticism ever
perpetrated in English letters. In 1818 he nursed his nineteen-year-
old brother Tom and watched him die of the tuberculosis that
would soon infect him himself. His passionate love for Fanny
Brawne shipwrecked on an utter lack of prospects, increasing illness, and his own temperament. During these last two years he
wrote his greatest poems. In the end, with his later poems unfinished and the plays never reached which he had hoped to write
in the wake of his adored Shakespeare, he was shipped off to Italy
by friends and well-wishers, in last desperate hopes for his health,
but to his own racking despair at the separation from his love which
he knew to be final. He died in Rome in the early spring of 1821,
before he had reached his twenty-sixth birthday. The sense of
defeat that would beset such a life as this is not hard to fill in.

He said towards the end that if he had had time he thought he
would have made himself remembered; and suggested his own
epitaph, "Here lies one whose name was writ in water."

Keats seems, in *The Fall of Hyperion,* to have been using in the
main two working-points from his life. The first is the agonizing
hypersensitivity of certain poetic temperaments (probably a sickness as Keats suggests in the poem, yet "sickness not ignoble") to
suffering in others and, though this is no more than hinted at, properly, during the poem, in oneself. There is a good deal of evidence
on this in his Letters. The second is the recurrence of encounters
with death, actual or in the form of separation and the demise
of dearest prospects in one's own or others' lives. I think Keats's
experience of love would rank here, so that it cannot enter separately as an ordeal that mediates vision in his own heroic quest.
Again the two points with which he is figuring are, in the poem,
the very points of transformation. We noticed that he was admitted
to the inner temple, vision within vision, on the first grounds, an
excessive capacity to suffer. So Moneta says:

> Only the dreamer venoms all his days,
> Bearing more woe than all his sins deserve.
> Therefore, that happiness be somewhat shared,
> Such things as thou art are admitted oft
> Into like gardens thou didst pass erewhile,
> And suffer'd in these temples . . .

Her note of disdainful tolerance reminds us of the weakness of
the poet, that essential weakness if there is to be vision or advance
at all. So we come to the second point, the recurrence of death
in this life, for it is, we remember, only through the three near-
deaths of the poem that any increase in the passionately pursued
visionary power is gained.

In each of the two heroic poems we have been considering, we found what seemed to be an over-all scheme, a network
of points of action common to both of them and suggesting other
such points in our great tradition of tragedy and tragic epic. It is
one thing to draw a scheme out of literary works, quite another

to draw one out of the vastly more complex matter of the human life. Yet if we look at these two lives, Milton's and Keats's, we may find that they too present certain characteristics or points of action which they hold in common. The quality in a life which Milton calls poem and Keats allegory must reside in some more formal similarity of this sort rather than in any particularity of detail.

What do these two very different lives have in common? The answer seems to be: conscious dedication of the life to poetry, seen as a total vocation although some form of human calling may, perhaps must, be practised as well; a marked degree of involvement, entailing openness and vulnerability to people and life at whatever level, public or private, family, friends, women; a great deal of suffering; and by the time death approaches, something like a spectacle or sense of failure.

May we now remind ourselves of the scheme which heroic poetry put before us? It was built up on the pursuit of some one energetic purpose, pursuit of vision, advance by a series of ordeals which were encounters with death, and suffering and weakness seen as essential points of operation, given the other condition of action and struggle, of advance in human power and insight.

The two are so close that we are justified in assuming in them that exactitude of relation which Mallarmé says is the essential basis of metaphor. The metaphor stands then: the individual life is (or can be) myth, allegory, heroic poem. This is not to make life into literature. It is to make all lives potentially into naked heroic suffering encounters with the universe.

The first thing to see is the importance of heroism, understood not as fanfare and triumph but as immense transformation of power at the point of weakness and pain. It is singled out by this formal scheme which has appeared here as common to poems and to lives, as a major point of human advance, in power and insight. "But must we not admit the part which heroic virtue plays in human evolution?" asks Dr. Needham in *Time the Refreshing River*, London, 1943. There is no relegating it to ancient days; it is as timely and urgent now as ever in the days of Hector or Samson, and as important for young people to know and reach out towards. For, if it is not restricted to past time, it is not restricted to exceptional persons either. Its very formalism, the bare bones of a scheme of human action and direction and suffering possible in any circumstances, opens it to anyone who chooses it. (This formalism is very interesting in itself; I wonder whether all myths might not in the end suggest themselves as basic and bare essences of human action and passion in the universe in this way, but clothed in a narrative morphology which provides the images for this use of the human metaphor?)

Any human being may, it seems, accept the invitation, dread and wonderful as it is, to live one's life as myth, the life of heroism which is somehow to advance our vision as human beings in this universe. The one condition seems to be the element, however dimly perceived, of choice, an act of will, consciousness at some level. Given some measure of consciousness of potential significance beyond itself, any life may offer itself into this metaphor, this skeleton scheme of operation which we flesh over with our own nerves and blood and life histories. Some establishment of the metaphor seems essential if life is to be lived to the full. This is why art in many forms offers the ordinary human being shape after shape of myth, with this pattern of suffering-which-is-effort or other equally vital patterns of our communal growth, with which to identify his own pattern of life, for growth and understanding. In religion the process holds yet more. It is noticeable how closely this heroic pattern fits the lives of the saints. In Christianity the establishment of the most intimate and loving relations possible between the individual life and the life of Christ is to lead ultimately, as in metaphor, to fusion. St. Paul grasps it firmly: "I live, yet not I but Christ in me." Only within such a pattern can human life reach its full development and move forward. Similarly, only within such an identification can religion, and myth, be at all understood, and this may be why in our time, when all the official methods of learning pull against such learning by identification, both have so little living justice done to them.

There remain two questions about the metaphor of the individual life as myth, allegory, poem. What is the force that shapes the life so that it can be thus compared with an art form? (This was Schopenhauer's great question, you recall.) And what is to be interpreted or divined by means of the metaphor once established?

The very size and enormity of the first question (Goethe says it is the principal riddle of the universe, which may well warn us off trying to answer it here) suggest that perhaps it is best not posed in quite these terms. Schopenhauer, in the essay of his which we have consulted, says that it cannot be even attempted by rational methods. Goethe agrees with him; in fact he gives this as the defining characteristic of that shaping force, whatever it may be, "a privily working power, a kind of fate" which, he says, is an inarticulable riddle of life and of the world, and which he names "das Dämonische." He and Eckermann were discussing it particularly during the early months of 1831. It is noticeable with what respect, one might say tentativeness, even this powerful mind approaches the question. He substantiates Schopenhauer's outline of its operation as part deep drive in human nature, part deliberate choice of the human will, part the congruent play of apparent accident. Like him too, he connects the last, the centre of the riddle, with nature, and with Providence, but differentiates it, as Schopenhauer also did, from both. For philosopher and poet, the postulated shaping process operates in a field where, as in the human mind itself, the division between what we call conscious and unconscious, between what we consider purposive and what we consider chance, necessary for our day-by-day practical operation, perhaps does not exist at all.

Schopenhauer says that, under his great myth of the *Wille,* we each of us will what happens to us, including accidents. There are indications in modern psychological knowledge that in part at least this is true. To take two cases that occur to me, there are the people who are accident-prone and who frequently seem to have some inner enjoyment of incapacity or failure, a connivance with the curious adventures which befall them. It is not merely that they are manually clumsy, or unobservant; that would be simple of explanation. They are "unlucky" as we say. To speak a little exaggeratedly, tiles wait for them to walk past underneath before they fall off the roof. There is a second indication of the same sort in the recent advances in understanding the role of the psychosomatic in diseases of the body. I think people will repudiate this way of thinking only if they have failed to observe the extraordinary and often alarming congruence between a human being's real and profound loves-and-hates and the life which, as we say, they make for themselves. What you want you may form or receive. It matters beyond expression to want, at the heart, what is living and right. The most daring and penetrating study of this that I know in modern literature is Ibsen's tragedy, *The Master Builder*. It is a superbly ambiguous title in itself. The architect who is the hero of the play was a genius, with a belief in daimonic "helpers" who shaped the ways of his life for him. Yet who really structured the action, in which he obtained his real latent wishes at the cost of suffering and death all round him? and finally his own defeat in the last ordeal and a death which yet in turn seems to be some dark illumination? Ibsen is at work, here as elsewhere in his drama, on the core of this problem, which has to do, whether in Schopenhauerian terms or not, with the will, and, whether in Freudian terms or not, for Freud will pick it up also, with a consciousness and direction in the human mind and the universe.

And this is as close as we can get to our second question: what is the individual human life as metaphor to explore or interpret? Consciousness, which seemed to be a condition for the metaphor's operation, may also indicate its field. It is helpful to distinguish in this respect between the field of the priestly, scientific and poetic dynasties respectively. In the holy life, it seems to me, the heuristic, if it can be thought of in such a way, is directed towards increasing knowledge of the relations possible between God and His creatures. In science (and the scientific life, too, for there is commitment here just as with saints and poets) the aim is the greater understanding of the natural universe. Poetry appears to hold a kind of middle ground between the two. It is not concerned with the natural world regarded as separate or severed off from human consciousness; nor is it directly and professionally concerned with the world of supernatural relations revealed by religion. In its narrative or living form which we have just been considering and perhaps in any of its forms, the human metaphor has to explore and interpret a universe in which human consciousness has supervened and of which it is a constituent part.

If it is possible to conceive of a line of interplay between the natural universe and that universe which opens with the advent of consciousness, this is where the poet is set. The representative simply of man as such, with sentient body, passionate mind and the gift of speech, he has the task that all men have though they do not always know of it: to act as the meeting-place and point of mutual conversion between the physical world, apparently inanimate, often intractable, and the world of mysterious appearances and powers which are not material, lie beyond the mind, and whose presence we all surmise unless we are totally bound within the physical world ourselves. (To think of a concrete poetic example may help here—*King Lear; The Ancient Mariner*; the Duino Elegies.) The particular task is to extend our consciousness at these crossing-points and to present the relationships thus apprehended in human terms. The poems are a part of this work. The life is, or can be, too.

One such crossing-point we have been looking at in this Chapter, heroic poem and heroic life which, says our metaphor, are so intimately connected as to be fused in this task of transformation. The working point of the metaphor was marked by the human experience of suffering, effort and weakness. We come now to a second such crossing-point. Its specific identification is again a cluster of universal human experiences. This time the human metaphor is working at the point of love and death.

Five

THE FIGURE OF LOVE
AND DEATH

I

THIS LAST FIGURE OF THE POETS THAT WE SHALL LOOK
at, love and death, or, as I prefer to write it here, love-and-death, is
not merely a figure in poetic method or a matter of literature. Admittedly, nothing in the human metaphor is, but this least of all. If a
note of urgency, such as we began this study with, came creeping
back into the last Chapter as we touched on our need of the heroic
as something challenging and within reach, that note is even clearer
with this new figure. I am convinced—and the conviction comes not
from theorizing but from moving about the world teaching and
writing poetry and fiction—that this figure of love-and-death, too, is
crucial in terms of human lives at the present time. We are confronted here perhaps more than anywhere else in the range of the
human metaphor at present with the intimate relation between our
ways of thinking and our image of man.

Love and death, separately, seem obvious enough subjects for
poets; at least, a great deal of poetry has been written on or around

156

them. But for the rest of us? And why the hyphening, the linking of them into love-and-death which may seem to us strange or even morbid? Yet what seems to us strange in cold print is in another context so familiar in our day-to-day lives that we scarcely even notice it any more. The merest glance at the world of popular culture in which we are all willy-nilly submerged discloses the degree to which all of us and particularly the young are obsessed by images of love and death in the elementary form of sex and violence, not separated but in some secretive yet blatant embrace. This is the world of images or fictions, but we know how it is answered by the world of real lives. Distorted form of love-and-death though sex-and-violence may be, they provide evidence of the connection, and of this pair as in some way essential to us beyond the solely physical. Indeed, our pursuit of them suggests a hunger amounting to starvation at this point.

Keeping this unliterary and very actual side of things in our minds, we can go on to look at a few aspects (to attempt more than this is impossible) of love and death as a particular working place in the human metaphor and the connection between them.

Sex and death are delivered to us by our bodily nature and heritage. They are part of our condition as living organisms, mere data or happenings, it might seem. Yet even in their non-human aspects, our thinking about them takes an interesting turn. Biologists tell us that they entered the world together in the history of living creatures, at the point of the differentiation of the individual and the development of sexual reproduction; and there has been for over 150 years a tendency among us to regard both sex and death, even at this point, as artifices of nature, cunning contrivances, artifacts. Paley calls sex "the grand relation of animated nature . . . subsisting like the clearest relations of art"; Erasmus Darwin considers it to be "the *chef d'oeuvre* of nature," while Teilhard de Chardin terms it "cette invention prodigieuse." The same metaphor, if that is what it is, appears in both Freud's and Shaw's discussion of the work of the biologist Weismann on life and death. Both, the one in *Beyond the Pleasure Principle,* 1920, the other in the Preface to *Back to Methuselah,* 1921, quote their original as saying that death is not a necessary condition of organic life but an "expedient." The word occurs in each. Even at the pre-human stage, love and death are being thought of in terms which approximate to those we were investigating as part of the human metaphor in the last Chapter, not so much an incident as a working-place.

At the physical level, sex and death have been felt for a very long time to possess a formal symmetry of dynamic the one to the other. The rhythm of sexual desire in human beings (as distinct from the specific periodicity in most animals) whose constant availability is one of our problems and perhaps also one of our great advantages is given in poetic imagery the rhythm of a death which is life-bearing for its metaphoric counterpart. The phoenix is used in this way, in Shakespeare's *All's Well That Ends Well,* for instance, in one of the most wonderful passages ever written on woman and love, where Helena describes to Parolles what a woman would wish to be to her beloved. She includes a phoenix in her list of attributes, an image we have already met in *Samson Agonistes,* for death and rebirth, some constant revivification which life obtains for itself in a pattern of crisis and renewal. (In the English language the connection became so close as to permit linguistic identity by the seventeenth century—possibly earlier for all I know. Certainly in Dryden's poetry the verb "to die" is in familiar use as an expression for female sexual orgasm. Freud comments on ."the likeness of the condition that follows complete sexual satisfaction to dying" in Chapter IV of *The Ego and the Id,* 1923).

At the social and organizational level of humanity they appear once again in connection. Historians derive man's earliest temporary settlements from these two, in their more institutional forms of marriage and begetting and of burial; and from this the whole development of city and state and all their institutions may follow.[1]

---

[1] In the *Scienza Nuova*, Vico speaks of "questi tre umani costumi: che tutte hanno qualche religione, tutte contraggono matrimoni solenni, tutte seppelliscono i loro morti." *Opere*, Milan, 1953, p. 480. Cf. also Lewis Mumford, *The City in History*, New York, 1961, p. 9, "But note that two of the three original aspects of temporary settlement have to do with sacred things, not just with physical survival: they relate to a more valuable and meaningful kind of life, with a consciousness that enter-

The fact that both were felt to be numinous, and the clustering of rite and taboo round the dead and their burial and round women and generation, are among the most characteristic signs of humanity. These two phenomena—as witness the mythic quality ascribed to them, which is also their speculative potential—must have seemed to us from the start capable of development as figures of the mind.

It has plainly been part of the central task, self-imposed, of our civilization to examine and develop the concept of love, not as private business of our own but as part of our contribution to humanity. The poets are deeply engaged in it and the imaginative structures they build up with it, as mental and living experiments, become patterns for wider human experience. "The common prejudice that love is as common as 'romance' may be due to the fact that we all learned about it first through poetry," Hannah Arendt says in *The Human Condition*; she continues, "But the poets fool us; they are the only ones to whom love is not only a crucial, but an indispensable experience, which entitles them to mistake it for a universal one." Ortega y Gasset in his wonderful little work *On Love*, published in translation in New York in 1957, says that "Love is a work of high art," and later adds, "Ignoring for the present the possible connection between love and certain cosmic instincts latent in our being, I think that love is indeed the complete opposite of an elemental force . . . I would say . . . that love rather . . . resembles a literary genre . . . not an instinct but rather a creation, and, in man, no primitive creation at that. The savage has no inkling of it, the Chinese and the Indian are unfamiliar with it, the Greeks of the time of Pericles barely recognized it." It is of the modern West, and it is this aspect of it which is discussed in such authoritative works as *Love in the Western World* by Denis de Rougemont and *The Allegory of Love* by C. S. Lewis. There is general agree-

---

tains past and future, apprehending the primal mystery of sexual generation and the ultimate mystery of death and what may lie beyond death . . . In the earliest gathering about a grave or a painted symbol, a great stone or a sacred grove, one has the beginning of a succession of civic institutions that range from the temple to the astronomical observatory, from the theater to the university."

ment that the Provençal poets of the eleventh century gave the first sudden yet decisive impetus to the resolve to explore in particular erotic love between man and woman, and from this point the enquiry goes forward without a break for close on a thousand years, to where we now find ourselves.

Scholars, it seems to me, tend to emphasize the arbitrariness of this eleventh-century turning point, and also, Christian scholars particularly, feel bound to suggest to us that this secular preoccupation of ours may be aberration. To a working poet in this tradition, however, the enquiry is a great mythological divining from sex and synthesis in physical structures into the organization of interpretative structures in the mind and life of man (the enquiry has run an interesting course in science), involving society, politics and religion. To a poet also, the great development of interest in love, which in the early Middle Ages in Europe turns to the relation between man and woman, was only the making actual of something inherent in our tradition from much further back, in the whole tenor of Greek myth, for instance, the cosmic Eros and the celestial Aphrodite whom Lucretius invokes, and, to turn to the other main root of our culture, in the extraordinary fact that Christianity identified God with this all-inclusive urge in the creature to unite with another object and to give itself wholly, in a range of experience which will include sexual functions, human relations, thought, and the most intense efforts of the divining soul. Once love is given this degree of pre-eminent significance, the rest follows.

I am using the word 'love' in the broadest sense it can have, as Freud, for his purposes, so repeatedly and rightly pleads that we must do when thinking of these matters. Attempts at differentiating between *kinds* of love, particularly in a religious context, seem always unhelpful. The lover loves entire. Only the expression takes different forms.

Less work has been done upon death. Norman Brown in *Life against Death*, Wesleyan University, 1951, says, "The elucidation of Freud's vision of organic life as a dialectical unity of life and death is hampered by the inadequacies in the current philosophy of organism. Psychoanalysis would like to start with a clear idea of the role of death at the organic level." I know of no scholarly studies of death comparable to those to which one can refer in the case of love. I shall begin, therefore, with the work on it, in modern times, that I know. We have glanced already at thinkers who were considering non-human death as an expedient. With this goes the idea of death as voluntary, an idea for which there is a certain amount of direct evidence incidentally in the fields of psychology, animal and human, medicine and anthropology. There is a suggestion of death, in the human being, as a matter of the will, in Edgar Allan Poe's story, *Ligeia*. The author puts at the head of this story a short quotation, or pastiche, from Joseph Glanvill: "And the will therein lieth, which dieth not. Who knoweth the mysteries of the will, with its vigour? For God is but a great will pervading all things by nature of its intentness. Man doth not yield himself to the angels, nor unto death utterly, save only through the weakness of his feeble will." This looks towards the work of Schopenhauer, with its notion of will and Will and their relation to death, the Schopenhauer whom we shall find Freud and Shaw quoting when they too take up this theme of death as voluntary, not involuntary. Shaw's play, *Back to Methuselah,* is the most developed discussion of this aspect of the theme we have so far had.

Death, like love, may also be regarded as something man-made— "Man has created death" as W. B. Yeats exclaims, in the little poem *Death* in *The Winding Stair,* 1933, contrasting man's death with the neutral death of the animal. Death is not simply artifice but artifact, and had already been seen so by Carlyle in *Sartor Resartus.* After the sentence quoted in the last Chapter where Carlyle spoke of the human life as a work of art, he goes on: "In Death too, in the Death of the Just, as the last perfection of a Work of Art, may we not discern symbolic meaning?" As so often, this great prophet reaches the centre at one bound: death is both the finishing touch to the life's work of art and an image for further divination.

In the poem of Yeats just mentioned there is an indication of the basis on which this kind of thinking depends. Yeats says of man, "Many times he died, / Many times rose again." The view of death as voluntary, as creation or work of art, depends on seeing it not as a single final catastrophe but as a recurring accompaniment and essential part of living. This is an old view. You may look for it in

Sir Thomas Browne, or in St. Paul. It makes a very close relation between death and life, some of the dynamic of which we have glimpsed already as at work in tragedy. It makes also a connection between the two themes with which we are immediately concerned, for it means that death, like love, permeates life and is not capable of being relegated to our last hours.

More recently there has come into the poetic dynasty a sense of urgency about this aspect, love and death, of the human metaphor, and the turning of a number of minds, and lives, towards this working-place. It begins, like so much else, in the late eighteenth century, and the special people are Novalis, Schopenhauer, Richard Wagner, Freud and Rilke.

There is an extremely close, almost genetic relationship between the members of this line, and a number of commentators point this out. Thomas Mann, for instance, in his essay of 1933, *Sufferings and Greatness of Richard Wagner*, makes Novalis a direct ancestor of Wagner's thought in *Tristan und Isolde*, while Novalis is again put forward by Norman Brown in *Life against Death* as at the root of the psychoanalytical approach pioneered by Freud. This author is particularly interesting because he includes Hegel too at this point: "The first break-through of the insight which flowers into psychoanalysis occurs in German idealism, in Hegel's notion of the world as the creation of spirit, and, even more, in Novalis' notion of the world as the creation of the magic power of fantasy." Thus also Schopenhauer in the same philosophic or poetic tradition, and *Welt* as *Vorstellung*. Brown also puts Hegel and Novalis among "the poets whom Freud credited with being the real discoverers of the unconscious"[2] and he goes on to suggest credentials for Hegel which might well include him in our genealogical table, "Of Hegel's two systematic attempts to grasp the essence of man, the first identified man with love and the second identified man with death . . . It was only in his second attempt . . . that Hegel was able to grasp man as

[2] This sentence as it stands in the original is ambiguous. I do not think the author means that Freud ascribed this thought to Novalis and Hegel in particular, but to poets in general. Thomas Mann says Freud did not know Novalis, but the context of his remark makes one unsure about it —see Footnote 5, p. 178.

essentially a history-making creature." Schopenhauer's connection
with Wagner is well known. The former's title-deeds in this line of
research are indicated by Thomas Mann in his essay, *Schopenhauer,
1938*: "He (Nietzsche) says that a man has the philosophy proper to
his years, and that Schopenhauer's world-poem has the stamp of
the time of life when the erotic predominates. And the feeling for
death, may one add." I am omitting further consideration of him here
not because he is unimportant but because he is out of my reach at
present, and the same is true of Wagner, who in any case would
reveal his central significance in a context other than a purely
poetic one. (I mean, of course, political, not just musical.) We have
already glimpsed the Schopenhauer-Freud connection and shall
return to this, and Norman Brown in that work of his already
quoted closes the series with Rilke, a poet whom he sees as expanding independently in his own work the insights which had
taken shape as psychoanalysis in the mind and discipline of Freud.

Out of this line, in which German thought predominates over the
rest of Europe with a kind of fateful significance yet to be explored,
we will take three individuals who work at this figure of love-and-
death. Novalis is the first, and we shall look at his *Hymnen an die
Nacht*, written in 1797. The second is Freud, with his two short
works, *Beyond the Pleasure Principle*, 1920, and *Civilization and its
Discontents*, 1930. The third is Rilke and the *Duineser Elegien*,
Duino Elegies, written from 1912 onwards and published in 1923.
Rilke is in certain ways the most immediately contemporary for
our purposes here, and we shall start with him, taking Freud second,
and ending with the young poet who, more essentially than the
other two, recalls us to our broader theme, for not only does he
deal in love-and-death but he lends his life to this figure, for the
better illumination of the human metaphor in this its ultimate form.

II

It may seem absurd to turn for help to poems reputed as dark
and difficult as the ten Duino Elegies are. But we are not going to
'interpret' them—this is no work of literary criticism—but to trace

out in them if we can, particularly in the First, Sixth and Tenth, the work to be done now on the point of love-and-death in the human metaphor and its connection with what has been done here by the poets before. For, it seems to me, this is what the Elegies are about.

The poems from the beginning indicate some great work which is now to be undertaken, unclear as yet even to the poet himself as he addresses himself to an overwhelming task. So the First Elegy begins with an image, new and yet very old, of wrestling with an Angel, and a great cry goes up from the human called to this. Gradually the nature of the work to be done, the transformation to be effected, begins to take shape. Already in line 36 the poet is saying to himself, "singe die Liebenden," sing the lovers . . . Here already, and crucially, is a suggested point where something is to be done, to be achieved. Then at once, in connection with his task which he gropes towards, and with the lovers, Rilke mentions the hero, "der Held"; he is involved too, in terms of death which is revivification, "seine letzte Geburt," the poem says. Thus love and death enter already, though so far separately. For the present, however, it is to the lovers that the poet turns, as if with special urgency. Here, he feels, is the point of questioning. Have we thought enough about past lovers, he asks, and ought not our past sufferings in this vein to be bearing more fruit? "Ist es nicht Zeit?" There is a work to be done here; in any case, as he says, standing still is impossible. Things have to become more than they now are (as the Angel is more than we). Love is, Rilke tells us, such a thing. The forms of love have to be struggled with and remade.

I do not mean this figuratively but literally, as Rilke did. He believed, as is clear from his Letters (like Keats he is a marvellous letter-writer), that love in our day must undergo some central transformation, become less sexually dialectical, more human. (See, for instance, the letters to Franz Xaver Kappus of July 16, 1903, and May 14, 1904). The poet is at work on love still, as he has been all along in our culture.

In the Second and Third Elegies Rilke shows us something of the effort to be put into this transformation of love and its direction. He sees it as part of our constant and obligatory human effort to draw significance from the facts of our living; love seems to afford some way beyond the merely transitory and accidental into the invisible and timeless, yet love as we experience it today, with all its sweetness, is simply not adequate for such a task of divining and interpretation. This is the note of the Second Elegy towards the end, and here the poet indicates, with two images and the quietness that is proper to a matter so vital not just for him but for all of us, the effort towards a change in love which he sees us as needing. The first image is that of the quiet restraint of the gestures of human figures on ancient Attic gravestones (sculpture always had power to move Rilke's mind); the hands rest gently on the other's body, as if love and farewell—the farewell which is death—were always one and the same, and the poet says that this self-mastery came from knowing where the human ended and the divine, which is fiercer and stronger and not our business, began. The second image he uses is that we should find for ourselves some narrow simple enclosed strip of fruit-bearing land, between the torrent and the granite, where we might live, and this he calls "the human," "ein reines, verhaltenes, schmales Menschliches." Long before, he had said this to Kappus in a letter, "to change the love relationship from its very foundations, to reshape it into a relationship which is directed towards relation between human and human and no longer between man and woman."

If this seems just didactic moralizing in a poet, consider first the beauty of the images and then our present condition in these matters. A plea against convulsiveness and lack of limits in love between man and woman, a plea for the human against the inhuman at this point—the poet is surely right that this is what we need, to judge by the spectacle which we in the West present as far as "love" is concerned. Is he not right, too, when he says, in a letter to Lisa Heise, January 19, 1920, on this same subject, "Unsere Traditione sind unleitend geworden"—our traditions have become 'unleading,' giving us no guidance any more, dead branches, Rilke adds, no longer nourished out of the roots' strength? What he sends us back to, in this letter and in the First Elegy, is death. "Only from the standpoint of death," as it runs in the letter, "provided one does not think of it as just a Being-Dead but gropes towards it as an intensity which surpasses us utterly, only from the standpoint of death can one get love straight." This was Rilke's conviction from the very first poems he wrote. This is his vocation or vision.

In the first major collection of poems which he published, *Das Stunden-Buch*, the third part, written in 1903, is called *Von der Armut und vom Tode*, of poverty and death. He shows how the great cities of today cheat their inhabitants of their life but also of their death; and he prays, "O Herr, gieb Jedem seinen eignen Tod"—give every man his own death, the dying which grows out of his individual life alone and which has for him love, significance and its own necessity. We shall need to remember this when we come to Freud. Through another fifty lines or so this early poem elaborates the idea of a death proper to each life, which each must ripen and with which he lives all through his life. Then the poet turns to the hero, though he is not yet called so, simply "One," or "the One"; in the poet's mind such a transformation of death can be achieved only by such a one. In him our miserable deaths are to be reborn glorified and it is the task of the poet to sing this—"Ich will ihn preisen."

This is one side of Rilke's way of thinking about death: that we each need and must move towards a death especially our own. The other is the interpenetration of the worlds of the living and the dead, not just metaphysically but physically, as in the poem *Orpheus. Eurydike. Hermes* of 1904, or the 1922 *Sonette an Orpheus*. The immediate presence of both realms is what he celebrates, as also the continual metamorphosis between the two. It is thus that he interprets suffering, death itself and those forms of death which we call by the lesser names of farewell, denial, renunciation, but which every truly living life knows for deaths when it meets them. Such a life may also know, however, as Rilke did, that they are in some strange way points of access of energy if built back into life again, incorporated and not convulsively ejected. Rilke speaks of this with great clarity and insight in a letter of September 11, 1919, to Adelheid von der Marwitz: "With every cheerful readiness to take hold, every glance forward and outward to the as yet untouched future, we transform not only the immediate present, moment by moment, we reshape also the past in us, weave it into ourselves, dissolve and absorb into us the foreign bodies of pain, that substance of which we do not know the composition nor how much, it may be, of added impulsion to life it may impart, in solution, to our blood. No death, not even the most deeply felt, is ever imposed as a protracted obstacle to living in the human who survives it, for its innermost being is not hostile to us but is, as one might often guess, more knowledgeable about life than we are in our most alive moments. I always think that its great weight, its enormous pressure, have in some way the task of forcing us downwards into a deeper and more inward stratum of life, in order that we may grow up out of it all the more fruitful. Circumstances gave me practice in this experience very early on, and it has been confirmed for me by sorrow after sorrow."

In the Elegies the poet hears first the voices of the young dead whispering to him; not those who died after a normal life-span but those who departed in the summer of life. It is we, Rilke says, who draw too sharp distinctions here; the Angels often do not know whether the humans they move amongst are living or dead. The dead speak to us, not because they have need of us—they have accomplished their task which is to free themselves gradually from the living, for in Rilke's thought death too is effort, "das Totsein ist mühsam"—but because we have need of them. They, like the lovers and the hero, know about suffering and its possible transformation into the bliss of advance.

In the Third Elegy the dead and the living meet, at the point of erotic love. Rilke here describes the man in the love partnership as compounded of the incredibly ancient, savage, often sinister stuff of all the dead of his line, the fierce old myths dwelling like gods in the rivers of his blood; and all of this unbelievable but totally real and actual inheritance rises, when love stirs, to meet the girl who will take it, all of it, in her arms, whether she has any inkling of it or not. We, in this vision, like a thought in Wordsworth's psychology, have no beginning, only an immemorial, anything-but-dead past, which we continue and which lives on in us. As the poet says to the girl, "How were you to know you had called up all of prehistory in your beloved?" The dead are active participants in every love between man and woman, and with this the woman must deal. The mother begins the task with her small son, then the woman who loves him must take it on, gentling all this ancientness into living humanity again.

The Fourth Elegy turns to death in childhood, the Fifth to a very

Parisian image of acrobats performing in the shoddy public square but in the poet's vision transfigured into lovers who show their dazzling and vertiginous art in a celestial city, watched and applauded by the surrounding dead. With this, the first movement of the Elegies is over.

The Sixth has for its subject the Hero. Rilke was thinking about him also in the beautiful *Fünf Sonette* of 1913. He appears there as a uniting of things we mistakenly hold to be opposites, and as the most telling example of faithfulness to a vocation. *Der Held, der Liebende, der Dichter,* hero, lover, poet, are concerned in this destiny which is presented as a fusion of life and death, but the vocation is not restricted to them; it is open, Rilke says, to anyone who will utter the word—"Herr, ich bin gewillt." When he returns to this subject in the Sixth Elegy, it cannot but delight us here that the figure he should choose to typify the Hero should be Samson. The poetic tradition holds good through the years, for Milton and Rilke are asking, through that figure, the same question, about the significance of the heroic life and of their own.

For Rilke, the Hero is essentially the embodiment of life-and-death seen as one single and self-renewing dynamic; not love-and-death. The Hero must rush to his destiny and can make no stay in the halts of love which is for him only another mode of his swift death-and-life transformations. He is another modulation of the youthfully dead, speeding into the invisible.

This theme of transformation is expanded in the Seventh to Ninth Elegies, the poet feeling his way back from the Hero, as in the First Elegy, to what seems to him more the centre of his task, the lovers and the dead. They are a vital part of the process by which earth is constantly rendered back into the more real invisible world, in which transformation, the vocation of poet and of everyman, death is a masterstroke of invention, Earth's sacred idea as the poem says.

The Tenth Elegy seems to gather up now not only Rilke's own thoughts but also a number of the images and pointers we have found in our search along this whole track of the human metaphor. It starts with a great paean, before the praising Angels, in praise of suffering, lest we waste it, try to get through with it, do not recognize it as part of our circling inner time and our dwelling place. There follows now an image of a city. Rilke calls it Pain City. It represents what we have made in the modern world of suffering and of love and death—I write them apparently here because in this context they are separate, obsessive, and ruined. We moderns emphasize love and death, but all distortedly, so that the fruitful place of suffering has become a cheap, noisy, shoddy Vanity Fair of a metropolis, an allegorical city which one recognizes at once as also wholly real; indeed one could name names for it over and over again in the West, were it not that to do so would be invidious. Chaffering market and stifling churches offering a cheap immortality and cash-down consolations; the carnival with seesaws of Freedom; Happiness as the one target at the shooting booths; obscene sideshows displaying the genitals and sex-behaviour of Money; the advertisement hoardings with their eternally-promising alcohol—this is real enough, in one sense; but it is not Rilke's sense nor, as we know, the one that matters. Walk through it, he says, slip through the planks, and there, absolutely next door, is the real world, of children and lovers and dogs. Here the country begins.

Yet this realer landscape, if I may use the phrase, is at once, also, a landscape of allegory. The young man who suddenly finds himself in it, after the terrible parody of suffering offered by the city, is both newly dead and a lover—the conditions of admission? He loves a girl, who guides him through this country because she is at home here; her name is a Lament. Affliction is here, tears, pain, enduring patience, all embodied in things of human life or landscape, and we may recognize once again the universe inner and outer, interchanging freely with itself as in Blake or Wordsworth. Indeed the pilgrimage the two figures take through this country becomes curiously Wordsworthian, for they go by night up into mountainous country and come in the end, in a narrow moonlit defile, to a gleam of water. It is the spring of Joy, and among men, the girl Lament says with reverence, it is a great and bearing stream. The young man, who is dead, is to go on, into the summit country of suffering-behind-suffering, *Ur-Leid*. (Were Ibsen's men in *Little Eyolf* or *When We Dead Awaken* exploring it?) He must say goodbye to the girl who weeps; here too as in all love for Rilke is the death of farewell. And the poem ends with his footfalls not even sending back an echo any more.

Keats surmised that the individual life was allegory and said of a being living such a life, "his works are the comments on it." In Rilke's thought, this extends also to the communal life. It seems that this too is allegory and our communal works are the comments on it. For him as for numerous thinkers in many other disciplines in this urban age, the city is central to his thinking. In this vision our modern cities are not merely the result but the actual taking-shape of what our minds and hearts are doing: "urban rot," "subtopia," the prestige and status factor, the exploding metropolis which is, Lewis Mumford says, the result of the "removal of quantitative limits."

This is Rilke's first great contribution to the work to be done on the human metaphor at its point of love-and-death in the individual and communal life. The second is his insistence that it is in fact because we have separated love from death and produced parodies of each in consequence that our plight, in our cities and elsewhere, is now becoming apparent. He shows us here, visibly, what happens to love without death, the death which is farewell, renunciation, control, suffering, limitation, and what happens to death without love, cheap, depersonalized, commercial, wasted. Here, this poet says, the work is to be done, on inward forms first in a reuniting of love-and-death and a transformation of them into something yet more human, yet more significant, in effort and suffering (for Rilke as for every poet effort is the condition of every advance). This is the point of transformation, of human advance in our time. Here our allegorical lives, of individual as of civilization, are to be reinterpreted and reformed.

III

When we turn to Freud's work[3] upon the love-and-death figure, it may seem to us, accustomed as we are to our rather rigid cate-

[3] Quotations in this section from *Beyond the Pleasure Principle* by Sigmund Freud by permission of Liveright Publishers, New York; from *The Ego and the Id* (1961) and *Civilization and its Discontents* (1962) by permission of W. W. Norton & Co., Inc. Numbered references relate to *The Standard Edition of the Complete Psychological Works of Sigmund Freud*, Hogarth Press, London.

gories, that we are moving into quite a different field; different in approach, activity and aims. In a sense, of course, this is true. It is helpful also, however, to keep before us the rather more flexible notion of the dynasties at work within a civilization as a whole, and their common task of working at man's image and his forms of thought and interpretation. In this context, and following on the poet's vision we began with, we shall perhaps be able to see more fully the significance of Freud's choosing to evaluate human life, first the life of the individual and then the life of the community, in terms of two great instincts to which he gave the names of Eros and death.

By the time Freud published *Beyond the Pleasure Principle* in 1920, the work in which he first clearly delineates his image of the two fundamental instincts in man, the life-instinct which he calls Eros, and the death-instinct, he had already established the doctrine and practice of psychoanalysis after a long battle. He had established them where he meant them to be, in that field of human endeavour labelled "Science." This small book of Freud's is not primarily a clinical work, however. It falls more into a category which Freud himself termed metapsychological, and Freud's biographer, Ernest Jones, tells us an interesting thing about it. After saying that "in dealing with such ultimate problems as the origin of life and the nature of death Freud displayed a boldness of speculation which was unique in his writing; nothing that he wrote elsewhere can be compared to it" (*The Life and Works of Sigmund Freud*, Vol. III, New York, 1957), Dr. Jones adds, "The book is further noteworthy in being the only one of Freud's which has received little acceptance on the part of his followers." A little later on he repeats, "the new theories met with a very mixed reception among analysts, and that in spite of Freud's high prestige" (pp. 266 ff.).

A reason for this may have emerged already out of what we have seen of Rilke's work. For the central work on love-and-death with which Freud associates himself definitely from 1920 onwards, and of which there are pointers much earlier in his thinking, is the occupation of the poetic dynasty. Thomas Mann, as we saw early in Chapter IV, claimed Freud as a fellow-worker in the poets' task of interpreting the individual life as myth. Now in this book of Freud's and the ones that follow it—*The Ego and the Id* of 1923, and *Civilization and its Discontents* of 1930—the psychologist declares himself as belonging right in the middle of the poets. To look only at Freud and Rilke, even apart from the other poets involved, seems to suggest one of the many fascinating cases of minds working simultaneously but independently of one another on a similar problem.

To regard Freud as a poet—we should at this point again recall that it is possible to belong to more than one dynasty—is nothing new. Where Thomas Mann, speaking in a literary context, calls him a writer of European rank together with Schopenhauer, and Norman Brown speaks of the "poetry," although in quotation marks, of Freud's thought, George Steiner in *The Death of Tragedy* says outright, "that great Jewish poet Freud"; best of all is the tribute paid by one authentic poet to another in W. H. Auden's poem, *In Memory of Sigmund Freud,* where after invoking the great myths to mourn, the living poet compares his dead co-worker to Dante, that is, sees in him an epic poet voyaging in his turn through a great other-world, also compounded of death and love.

The reckoning of him, in these terms and in any detail, is still all to do. We shall take here only an aspect or two according to our own limited purposes. We are going to begin with the long footnote which appears at the end of *Beyond the Pleasure Principle* and which summarizes much of the new thought in that work. Freud says:

> I will add a few words to clarify our terminology, which has undergone some development in the course of the present work. We came to know what the 'sexual instincts' were from their relation to the sexes and to the reproductive function. We retained this name after we had been obliged by the findings of psycho-analysis to connect them less closely with reproduction. With the hypothesis of narcissistic libido and the extension of the concept of libido to the individual cells, the sexual instinct was transformed for us into Eros, which seeks to force together and hold together the portions of living substance. What are commonly called the sexual instincts are looked upon by us as the part of Eros which is directed towards objects. Our speculations

have suggested that Eros operates from the beginning of life and appears as a 'life instinct' in opposition to the 'death instinct' which was brought into being by the coming to life of inorganic substance. These speculations seek to solve the riddle of life by supposing that these two instincts were struggling with each other from the very first. (Vol. XVIII, pp. 60 ff.)

This is a good survey of the expansion of what we are here calling "love" in Freud's thought (and what a developing, groping, often self-contradicting thought it is, as can be heard even in the above passage!) from physical sex-functions into some all-pervading principle of living matter; Freud refers in the text at this point to biology and the need for further enlightenment from this source. It is, indeed, the cosmic Eros of myth; Brown quotes Freud as saying, "The instincts are mythical beings, superb in their indefiniteness." According to Ernest Jones the same is true of the postulated death instinct as well. In Vol. III, p. 272, of his biography of Freud he says, "Freud's death instinct was not at all limited to mental aims; it was supposed to operate throughout the whole of living nature, and indeed perhaps in inorganic nature as well (radium!). With such a cosmic principle in his mind . . ." It seems that the final words of Freud's note, "from the very first," may be taken literally as summing up his view of the universe as some primal and never-ending agon between Eros and death . . . *Mors et vita duello conflixere mirando* as it runs in a different but not irrelevant context.

That this is a poetic and mythical vision, and that Freud in his own way knew it to be so, can be seen from this passage itself and its context. He embarks on this description of his vision because he wants to clarify the terminology, that is, the words. (Freud's whole relationship to words, active in the mind, from their ways in the less conscious levels right through to his views on "our god *Logos*" who appears in *The Future of an Illusion*, 1927, needs thinking about.) In the penultimate paragraph of *Beyond the Pleasure Principle*, just before the long note appears, he speaks of the obscurity in the vision, and proposes a patience, or as Keats would say, a negative capability, towards it: "This is merely due to our being obliged to operate with the scientific terms, that is to say with the figurative language, peculiar to psychology (or, more precisely, to depth psychology)." The equation of scientific terms and figurative language is flat and unequivocal, and lest we should think he does not mean it, he repeats it a sentence or two later in connection with physiological or chemical technical terms. He feels they might be better, as simpler and more familiar, but of them also he adds, "It is true that they too are only part of a figurative language."

The poetic and mythic approach is in his vision of Eros and death pervading the universe and the willingness to commit himself to a speculative working with figures, whether in science or elsewhere. But this approach is also to be seen in the man's life, as if here too he must join the poets in figuring not just with his mind but with the whole of himself. Of Eros in Freud's own life there must have been much; no one could so interpret the world without awareness within him of the full range of that great driving force. What is interesting is that there is unimpeachable evidence that death held no less intimate and impelling an influence in Freud's whole temper. Ernest Jones in Vol. III, p. 279, of his biography says, "As far back as we know anything of his life he seems to have been prepossessed by thoughts about death, more than any other great man I can think of except perhaps Sir Thomas Browne and Montaigne . . . He once said he thought of it every day of his life, which is certainly unusual. On the other hand there was a still more curious longing for death." Curious from the psychoanalytical viewpoint it may be, but not from the poetic. Here is another poet who, like Rilke, began as he meant to go on, and had his self-chosen place in the pulses of his own time from the beginning of his vocation.

Love-and-death, for Freud, takes the form of a battle between two forces. We should not be misled by this into thinking that we are faced with the ruinous separation of the two which, we suggested, our modern age has managed to accomplish. There are few relations closer than those of battle, except perhaps those of love itself, and Freud has often enough emphasized the frequent ambivalence of the two. Only from this point of view shall we understand what is going on. In *The Ego and the Id,* Chapter IV, Freud says that "life itself would be a conflict and compromise between these two trends," while the fact that he postulates both as within each organism, indeed within each single cell of that organism, should ensure our seeing them as related to one another, constantly and inseparably. That Freud sees primarily a dialectic or struggle at this point means, I think, that he is an epic poet, as Auden has already suggested to us, rather than a lyric one as Rilke is. To see what happens to this same love-and-death struggle when it becomes dramatic, one may turn to another poet in the dynasty, Shaw, and look at the superb duel Eros and death, in the persons of Don Juan and the Devil, hold in the great dream sequence set, like a scherzo, into the classical structure of Man and Superman, 1903.

Freud is considering not merely the relatedness but the identity of love-and-death already in 1913, in his essay, The Theme of the Three Caskets, and in a context of dramatic poetry, for the caskets are, of course, those of The Merchant of Venice where Shakespeare employs the old fairy-tale device of three rival suitors for a girl's hand, the bridegroom to be he who chooses the "correct" casket of the three which are made of gold, silver and lead. It is the leaden casket which is the right choice. This cannot but seem, to imagination and common sense, a patent inversion, and Freud, commenting on this very fact, unites the three caskets with the Three Fates, of whom the youngest was the fatal one, holding the power of death. At this point the substitution which yet implies identity takes place, according to Freud:

> So his imagination rebelled against the recognition of the truth embodied in the myth of the Moerae, and constructed instead the myth derived from it, in which the Goddess of Death was replaced by the Goddess of Love and by what was equivalent to her in human shape. The third of the sisters was no longer Death; she was the fairest, best, most desirable and most lovable of women. Nor was this substitution in any way technically difficult: it was prepared for by an ancient ambivalence, it was carried out along a primeval line or connection which could not long have been forgotten. The Goddess of Love herself, who now took the place of the Goddess of Death, had once been identical with her. Even the Greek Aphrodite had not wholly relinquished her connection with the underworld . . . (Vol. XII, p. 299).

From this point Freud moves on to consider King Lear, the three daughters of the king being variants of the same theme, an identification which makes Cordelia, most interestingly one feels, into love-and-death. Freud explains what he calls the overpowering effect this play has on us by saying that in it we hear this very note of profound myth that is being worked with and worked on, and in doing so gives us a lovely example of a poet turning back to a great predecessor and re-interpreting that ancestor's work in terms of his own vocation as he sees it in modern times.

Freud has given us, in the footnote already cited which concludes *Beyond the Pleasure Principle*, a good description of his developing views of love. He is much less expansive on the subject of the death instinct. He wrestles with this concept of his. Elsewhere, in *The Ego and the Id*, he says that the instinct relating to Eros is much more plastic and ubiquitous than that of death or destruction (Chapter IV), while later he calls the death instinct powerful but mute (Chapter V). He makes tentative connections between the death instinct and destructive or aggressive tendencies in the ego, introducing also the now well-known connection between Eros and cruelty or sadism, to which Nietzsche gave so much thought, although both Nietzsche and Freud are anticipated here by Novalis who establishes this relationship in two of his *Fragmente* of the 1790's.[4] On the whole, however, his thought on the nature of the death instinct, in *Beyond the Pleasure Principle* especially, is speculative and groping; as with all poets, Freud's best work is not that where he feels he can set down a Q.E.D.; and in the very questioning of his method, his trial of analogies only to drop them again, his development of an issue to its limit, reasonable or unreasonable, his frankness about his own position—"I do not know how far I believe in them"—are the most far-reaching insights and poetic connections to be found.

There is then a progression in Freud's thought. He himself outlines it for us from time to time, as for example at the end of *Beyond the Pleasure Principle*. He speaks there of three stages in his thought about instincts. The first was the recognition of the part played,

4 "It is curious that the association of sexual pleasure, religion and cruelty did not long ago make people aware of their intimate relationship and their common tendencies."

"Curious that cruelty actually derives directly from sex."

throughout life, by sex. The second was what Freud calls, again using myth for his terminology, "the hypothesis of narcissism," or self-love. The third is the hypothesis he has just put forward in this work, of two conflicting instincts, Eros and death. From now on he will develop this third stage, the love-and-death dialectic, and here too a shaped progression seems observable. In *Beyond the Pleasure Principle* he pays most attention to the physical, to matter or bodies and love-and-death working at that level. In *The Ego and the Id,* three years later, he is discussing more particularly "dynamic relations within the mind" as he says, and the dialectic or battle moves in there. Then in *Civilization and its Discontents,* seven years later again, the area of gaze expands once more, and the battleground of the two instincts now becomes coextensive with the whole of culture.

Beyond the Pleasure Principle, like so much poetic work, is at once innovation and development of latent tendencies present far earlier in the thinker's mind. James Strachey, editing this little treatise, indicates pointers towards it in Freud's writings as early as 1895. None the less it is expansion and exploration. The German title make this plainer than does the English version. *Jenseits* is of course 'beyond' but the German carries with it the implication of "on the farther side of," "on *that* side, not this." Freud tells us at the start that it is a basic tenet of psychoanalysis that the psyche automatically seeks pleasure and avoids or tries to reduce unpleasure: this is the pleasure principle. It is this very tenet, largely of his own constructing, that he wants to go beyond and to study "the operations of tendencies *beyond* the pleasure principle, that is, of tendencies more primitive that it and independent of it" (Vol. XVIII, p. 17). This is, as it follows and as we shall in fact see, to turn to the places where the mind works with and on pain. Freud's method is to marshal the evidence in the first three of the six Chapters, and then to introduce Chapter IV and what follows with the announcement: "What follows is speculation, often far-fetched speculation."

The evidence he adduces comes from three principal sources, all connected with the human tendency not to let past experiences of suffering alone, but to repeat them, in dreams, in the neurotic's compulsions, in the play of children. By the end of Chapter II these three have coalesced in his thought into the great human form which unites all of them, that is, drama. He raises the question of plays which "do not spare the spectators (for instance, in tragedy) the most painful experiences and can yet be felt by them as highly enjoyable." He describes them as "ways and means . . . of making what is in itself unpleasurable into a subject to be recollected and worked over in the mind," what we have called working-places; but because they give enjoyment and are within an aesthetic framework he regards them as still under the dominance of the pleasure principle, and not yet, therefore, his real subject matter. He has to penetrate deeper into the mind's doings.

In Chapter III accordingly he moves on from the figures in drama to consider figures in the real lives of normal individuals, certain patterns of experience which repeat themselves in the lives of some people though not all. Of these he says, "The impression they give is of being pursued by a malignant fate or possessed by some 'daemonic' power." It is this repeating pattern, so apparently inexplicable as to "give the appearance of some 'daemonic' force at work" or to present a "hint of possession by some 'daemonic' power" as he reiterates twice over at the beginning of the crucial Chapter V, which Freud singles out for special attention.

We are bound now to recapitulate and anticipate a little. Dream and drama as images for something happening in the human life, "apparent design in the fate of the individual"—we are back with the Schopenhauer whose essay, or 'speculation' as he chose to call it, we looked at in our last Chapter, and if we are not to be under a misapprehension we must also look forward to Chapter VI of *Beyond the Pleasure Principle* in which Freud mentions this philosopher and quotes briefly from him. The bibliographical footnote says, somewhat anonymously, Vol. V of Schopenhauer's Works. When we look into it, however, we find the reference is in fact to the very same essay of Schopenhauer's that we have been concerned with.[5]

[5] In *Freud and the Future* Mann says of Freud, "he did not know Schopenhauer." This is hard to understand especially since Mann elucidates Freud's thought by means of this very essay of Schopenhauer's which Freud quotes from.

These two great minds are at work together upon the problem of the force which appears to give perceptible pattern in individual human lives.

Freud says of it, "Psychology has always taken the view that their fate is for the most part arranged by themselves and determined by early infantile influences." He recognizes, however, as did Schopenhauer and Goethe too when confronting this question, the difficulties in an over-rational approach to it. It is the fact that the accidents seem to fit in which is the puzzle. Freud cites the case of the woman "who married three successive husbands each of whom fell ill soon afterwards and had to be nursed by her on their death-beds." (He adds that the most moving picture of this type of experience is to be found in Tasso's romantic epic, *Gerusalemme Liberata*.) He puts his finger on the difficulty: "This 'perpetual recurrence of the same thing' causes us no astonishment when it relates to *active* behaviour on the part of the person concerned . . . We are much more impressed by cases where the subject appears to have a *passive* experience, over which he has no influence, but in which he meets with a repetition of the same fatality" (p. 22).

It is typical of Freud that the explanation he has so far given should seem to him still only partial: "their fate is *for the most part* arranged by themselves"; "*a great part* of what might be described as the compulsion of destiny seems intelligible on a rational basis; so that we are under no necessity to call in a new and mysterious motive force to explain it" (My italics). Accordingly he prepares to go further: "Enough is left unexplained to justify the hypothesis of a compulsion to repeat—something that seems more primitive, more elementary, more instinctual than the pleasure principle which it over-rides." Freud has arrived at length at the point of passage to that other side, the *Jenseits* in the mind, where beyond all the rational explanations and their validity his own great myths wait for him.

Drawing a formal principle out of the pattern of repetition which he has been observing, Freud suggests that we consider this pattern "a universal attribute of instincts and perhaps of organic life in general," and draws from this a hypothesis: that an instinct is "an urge inherent in organic life to restore an earlier state of things." Or, as he rephrases it a little later, "all the organic instincts are conservative." This is speculation, we must remember, not biological history, and he carries it to its logical conclusion. Inanimate existed before animate: therefore all life, on this view, desires to return to the condition of inanimate matter, that is, to die. *"The aim of all life is death,"* Freud says (pp. 37-38).

Here, of course, is the death instinct. Freud immediately begins wrestling with the difficulties in such a view. What about the instincts for self-preservation in the organism? He suggests this answer, "They are component instincts whose function it is to assure that the organism shall follow its own path to death, and to ward off any possible ways of returning to inorganic existence other than those which are immanent in the organism itself . . . What we are left with is the fact that the organism wishes to die only in its own fashion." To each living thing, including each human individual, its own death—the thought is exactly that of Rilke in his *Stunden-Buch* days: "gieb Jedem seinen eignen Tod." Yet for Freud as for the poet, this is only half the story, and he at once begins to redress the balance by turning to the sexual instincts; not death only, but love-and-death.

Of the sexual instincts Freud says, "They are the true life instincts." I think, to use a phrase of his own, it astonishes us far too little that he should so absolutely have fused life and love. There is no external necessity to do so, although it is inherent in the Western tradition to which Freud so wholeheartedly belongs. Death for him is death plain and simple;[6] but life is Eros—the great name appears first in Chapter V in the last paragraph which is an interpolation of 1923. Freud sees the sexual instincts as also conservative in that they bring back earlier states of living substance, are peculiarly resistant to external influences, and preserve life itself over longer periods. In his thought they are the counterpoint to the death instinct, and he sees the individual life of the organism as a rhythmic pattern deriving from the opposition of the two. Speculation this still may be at this point, but it is nevertheless the shape that all of Freud's thought will take from now on.

[6] Ernest Jones in Vol. III of his biography of Freud says that it is odd that Freud never, except in conversation, used the term *Thanatos* for death.

Chapter VI concludes with an antiphonal shape of its own, for here Freud turns to biology for enlightenment on the phenomena of death and sex and turns back, expressing wonder ("we may be astonished to find how little agreement there is among biologists on the subject of natural death and in fact that the whole concept of death melts away in their hands"; "science has so little to tell us about the origin of sexuality that we can liken the problem to a darkness into which not so much as a ray of a hypothesis has penetrated") towards the two other dynasties with whom he sees his thought as coinciding: "In this way the libido of our sexual instincts would coincide with the Eros of the poets and philosophers which holds all living things together." The first poet-philosopher to enter is Schopenhauer, at the close of the rather abortive discussion on biological death which Freud concludes with these words, "We have unwittingly steered our course into the harbour of Schopenhauer's philosophy. For him death is the 'true result and to that extent the purpose of life,' while the sexual instinct is the embodiment of the will to live" (pp. 49-50). Then after questioning biology on sex, Freud turns to another poet-philosopher, to the *Symposium* and the myth which Plato there puts into the mouth of Aristophanes where erotic love is figured as the result of the gods splitting in two what had originally been a single human organism, and now each half goes endlessly seeking its other half. Freud moves among figures all the way through this last Chapter. He speaks halfway through of his postulate of the two conflicting instincts as "an equation with two unknown quantities," the mathematical figure. A little later, after citing the Platonic myth, he says, "Shall we follow the hint given us by the poet-philosopher, and venture upon the hypothesis ..." (p. 58). And later he writes the extraordinary lines I have already quoted, about scientific terms being in fact figurative language, just as another poet-philosopher, Coleridge, says that hypotheses are metaphors.

With *The Ego and the Id* we shall not stay long. Interesting and important as are the main lines of Freud's thought here, including the division of the mental life into ego, id and super-ego, and the consideration of guilt and its operations and significance within the self, these do not concern us directly. In the last two Chapters Freud develops his ideas on the two sets of instincts. In this work the death instinct appears primarily as sadism and the instinct for destruction, whether self- or other-directed. Similarly the concept of Eros is developed here, and what Freud calls the reservoir of displaceable, neutral energy in the mind, whether in ego or id, is held to be desexualized Eros, to which Freud adds, "If thought-processes in the wider sense are to be included among these displacements, then the activity of thinking is also supplied from the sublimation of erotic motive forces." (Vol. XIX, p. 45. Novalis preceded him here.[7]) There is an interesting discussion of death, in certain cases, as the ego's giving up the unending struggle to love itself, when "it lets itself die"—the idea of the voluntary death we have met already among the poets. The work ends with a last look at the mysterious inarticulate id:

> It cannot say what it wants, it has achieved no unified will. Eros and the death instinct struggle within it . . . It would be possible to picture the id as under the domination of the mute but powerful death instincts, which desire to be at peace and (prompted by the pleasure principle) to put Eros, the mischief-maker, to rest; but perhaps that might be to undervalue the part played by Eros.   (p. 59)

On that open note, the book ends. Eros is the tension-maker, the stirrer-up of work and trouble, struggle and effort, antipathetic here to the pleasure principle, yet, as Freud says in a later footnote (1923) to Chapter V of *Beyond the Pleasure Principle,* regarding the instincts he calls Eros, "it is to them alone that we can attribute an internal impulse towards 'progress' and towards higher development!" Here he was considering their dialectic in the dark world of the self. Now in his next work the process comes out into the world of society.

The tracing of the love-and-death instincts in physical matter and the body in *Beyond the Pleasure Principle,* then in the mind in

---

[7] "The life or essence of the mind consists in begetting, giving birth to and training up its own likeness"; "The organs of thought are the world's members of generation, the sex organs of Nature"—from the *Fragmente.*

The Ego and the Id, is well-connected and coherent. The jump now to *Civilization and its Discontents* seems far bigger. Freud himself utters exclamations of discouragement on this very point from time to time in the last-named work: yet in fact the organic unity and development of his thought holds good. He makes this plain to us, if only half-consciously, in the first Chapter by means of an image.

Freud is, as we should expect, a great maker of metaphors, and this one, extended and beautiful as it is, is typical rather than exceptional, not only as indicating Freud's methodology but also in its content. It puts before us the metaphor: the mind is a city, the city is a mind. The *civitas* or city-state of which we are citizens is not something other than and totally apart from our mind. It is the product of what moves in the mind; more than this, it is the actual image of it, as Blake and Rilke have seen particularly among the poets, and as Lewis Mumford understands. If we proceed to the fusion which metaphor entails, mind and city are one.

It is noticeable how often Freud employs civic or political imagery for mental events. One recalls the dream censor in *The Interpretation of Dreams,* the comparison of the ego first to a constitutional monarch, then to a time-serving politician, in Chapter VII of *The Ego and the Id;* or a later example again in *Civilization and its Discontents,* Chapter VII, where the moral conscience in civilized man's mind is compared to "an agency within him to watch over it, like a garrison in a conquered city" (Vol. XXI, p. 124. There are considerable divinatory possibilities in this metaphor for the exploration of politics).

The point Freud wishes to illustrate, in this section of *Civilization and its Discontents,* is what he calls the problem of conservation in the mind—"that in mental life nothing which has once been formed can perish—that everything is somehow preserved and that in suitable circumstances . . . it can once more be brought to light" (p. 69). He is thinking about the simultaneity within the mind of what is past and what is present, and has just cited examples of those in whom such a condition is clearly visible, the lunatic and the lover. To illustrate his thought, and as if to include the third of Shakespeare's trio, the poet, Freud turns to poetry or to an image, that of the city of Rome, the Eternal City as he calls it here. He describes the marvellous piled-up chaotic continuity of Rome's architecture, then says, "Now let us, by a flight of imagination, suppose that Rome is not a human habitation but a psychical entity with a similarly long and copious past" (p. 70). Here follows an astonishing elaboration of a shining translucent city, all its past edifices visible in and through the more recent ones, the dimension of serial time abolished in a superb image of simultaneity and interpenetration of structures in space. It is, as all good metaphor is, irrationally exciting.

Not the least interesting thing about the image is that it is framed in apologies. Freud is from the start a little deprecating about including this aspect of his subject matter—the conservation of levels of experience in the mind—at all. At the end, after he has described ancient Rome and made the "flight of imagination" which forms the metaphor, he turns away from what he has been doing: "There is clearly no point in spinning our phantasy any further . . . Our attempt seems to be an idle game." In the next paragraph, however, we find him discussing seriously whether the history of a city can be likened to the history of the mind, in view of the similarity or dissimilarity of the destructive agencies at work in each. He concludes against it—"a city is thus *a priori* unsuited to a comparison of this sort with a mental organism" (p. 71). Now any writer knows that if something proves really unsuited to one's argument, one does not say so and leave it in; one takes it right out and begins again. Yet the mind-city image stands here, as plainly as the fact that its author is in two minds about it, suggesting that in fact the metaphor does work at some level, though not at the common-sense one which Freud appears to try to withdraw to. The city-state is the mind: this is the foundation for the whole of his later discussion, in Chapters VI to VIII, of the role played in the city, or call it civilization from our Latin roots in the *civitas,* by the deep forces in the mind, his twin deities of love-and-death. In calling them deities I am not being fanciful. Freud's own language, in speaking about them, moves steadily in this direction.

Chapters VI and VII form a kind of unit on the subject of love-and-death, with Chapter VIII as an epilogue or last chorus. Chapter VI begins with a poet and psychoanalysis side by side. Of the latter,

Freud says, "Of all the slowly developed parts of analytic theory, the theory of the instincts is the one that has felt its way the most painfully forward" (p. 117). He then says, "I took as my starting-point a saying of the poet-philosopher, Schiller, that hunger and love are what moves the world." At the end of Chapter VII another poet-philosopher, Goethe, is quoted (Shakespeare is in a footnote early in Chapter VIII) and Freud comments, "And we may well heave a sigh of relief at the thought that it is nevertheless vouch-safed to a few to salvage without effort from the whirlpool of their own feelings the deepest truths, towards which the rest of us have to find our way through tormenting uncertainty and with restless groping" (p. 133). Freud seems to underestimate the efforts of poets at least in such a quest; but the sense of solidarity between the two or the three dynasties—or the one dynasty if all are poets as may be true—is remarkable. In this framework Freud speaks of Eros and Death, summarizing their progress in his thought hitherto and intro-ducing them now once again in their new context.

Having looked at the two earlier works on the subject, we need not go over again Freud's history of his thinking about the two in-stincts. There is a change to be noted, however. What were for him hypotheses earlier have now become convictions: "To begin with it was only tentatively that I put forward the views I have developed here, but in the course of time they have gained such a hold upon me that I can no longer think in any other way. To my mind, they are far more serviceable from a theoretical standpoint than any other possible ones; they provide that simplification, without either ignoring or doing violence to the facts, for which we strive in scien-tific work" (p. 119). Freud speaks of it as a scientific development in his mind; yet the reader may see it in terms a little different. The progress from hypothesis to conviction appears to be also that from metaphor to myth. Freud speaks now of his two instincts in a dif-ferent tone, one which befits the gods. It can be heard already when he is speaking of "the power of Eros" in contradistinction to "the energy of the death instinct," and is caught again audibly in the first great description of civilization seen from the point of view of "the eternal struggle between Eros and the instinct of destruction or death" (p. 132), a phrase which appears with slight modifications

twice at the end of Chapter VII. The following noble statement is
how Chapter VI draws to a close:

> In all that follows I adopt the standpoint, therefore, that the in-
> clination to aggression is an original, self-subsisting, instinctual
> disposition in man, and I return to my view that it constitutes the
> greatest impediment to civilization . . . Civilization is a process
> in the service of Eros, whose purpose is to combine single human
> individuals, and after that, families, then races, peoples and na-
> tions, into one great unity, the unity of mankind. Why this has
> to happen, we do not know; the work of Eros is precisely this
> . . . But man's natural aggressive instinct, the hostility of each
> against all and of all against each, opposes this progress of civi-
> lization. This aggressive instinct is the derivative and the main
> representative of the death instinct which we have found along-
> side of Eros and which shares world-dominion with it. And now,
> I think, the meaning of the evolution of civilization is no longer
> obscure to us. It must present the struggle between Eros and
> Death, between the instinct of life and the instinct of destruction,
> as it works itself out in the human species. This struggle is what
> all life essentially consists of. . . .   (p. 122)

It is an epic vision, no matter how unassumingly presented,
which emerges from these last chapters. A synoptic history appears
before us, exhibiting both continuity and conflict, with mythological forms ascribed to the forces operating there. Thus Freud says,
"The process of civilization is a modification which the vital process
experiences under the influence of a task that is set it by Eros and
instigated by Ananke—by the exigencies of reality" (p. 139), and he
realizes that it is this struggle which he has been seeking to interpret all along (as did Bergson and Shaw in their respective
vocations as poet-philosophers). Yet not only the continuity, the
conflict goes forward also. Indeed the continuing battle of love-and-
death *is* the life-process in Freud's thought, as the last sentence of
the passage quoted above explicitly says: "This struggle is what
all life essentially consists of." Life itself is Eros and Death in
mortal combat: life is love-and-death. This is Freud's epic version
of the human metaphor.

We saw that at the beginning of this treatise of his, Freud began
with the image of a city, and made this a metaphor for mind, an

eternal city in its continuity yet with a turbulent history of sack and violence. Through this image he joins Rilke in the Tenth Duino Elegy, begun eighteen years and finished eight years before *Civilization and its Discontents* was published. Like Rilke also, through this image Freud crosses over from considering the individual mind to considering that of the community, culture or civilization. In one major respect, however, the two differ. Rilke's vocation is lyric, and he works at love-and-death as a point of transformation and suffering in some heartfelt yet ultimately lonely heuristic of articulate intelligence and sensitive heart. Freud, on the other hand, is called not to lyric but to moral epic, and he sets the continuity and conflict of love-and-death, which for him is synonymous with life, fair and square in the moral conscience, whether of the individual or of society.

The discussion of the human conscience, the sense of guilt and its relation to punishment, the setting up of standards of conduct, occupies much of this book of Freud's. It belongs in the centre of his theme as is stated in Chapter VII, "for the sense of guilt is an expression of the conflict due to ambivalence, of the eternal struggle between Eros and the instinct of destruction or death" (p. 132). It begins, Freud says, as soon as we have to live with our fellows; first in the family—and he cites his great myth of love-and-death between parents and child, the Oedipus figure—then in society. Conscience is the weapon used by Eros to subjugate or divert the death-dealing and deadly instinct, turning the latter away from external manifestations hostile to Eros' work of binding men together, back into the individual personality. The harm which this may do, the havoc and danger caused by our souls being a battleground for titanic powers in this way, drew Freud's attention and his compassion all his life. In the city of the mind there is continual struggle. I quoted earlier a brief occurrence of the city image besides the main one in this work, a city subdued and garrisoned, watched over by a vigilant institution; that institution, we may now notice is, in Freud's metaphor, the moral conscience itself. One cannot help being reminded of another great figure, the citadel of Mansoul and the holy war which Bunyan told us of.

Freud begins with the image of a city, as do Gilgamesh and

Aeneid. For him it was the image of the human mind where conscience is the garrison and police of Eros against the forces of
Death. As he moves on to consider the mind of a community or
civilization, the city-state, his gaze directs itself more towards those
two immortal powers themselves who move and struggle through
it, as Ishtar raged in Uruk, or as Neptune and Juno and Athene and
not the Greeks battered Troy to ruin before Aeneas' startled, suddenly opened eyes. Freud's closing figure in this work is that of
invisible seraphic single combat, Love and Death

> addressed for fight
> Unspeakable; for who, though with the tongue
> Of Angels, can relate, or to what things
> Liken on Earth conspicuous, that may lift
> Human imagination to such highth
> Of Godlike Power; for likest Gods they seemd,
> Stood they or mov'd, in stature, motions, armes
> Fit to decide the Empire of great Heav'n.

That of course is the duel of seraphs in *Paradise Lost,* and Bunyan's
and Milton's relevance here suggests that we might think of Freud as
a great Puritan poet in this tradition; Shaw, with his clear-sighted-
ness, claims just this ancestry for himself. Now for Freud himself
on this theme, the closing paragraph of *Civilization and its Discontents:*

> The fateful question for the human species seems to me to be
> whether and to what extent their cultural development will suc-
> ceed in mastering the disturbance of their communal life by the
> human instinct of aggression and self-destruction. It may be that
> in this respect precisely the present time deserves a special in-
> terest. Men have gained control over the forces of nature to such
> an extent that with their help they would have no difficulty in
> exterminating one another to the last man. They know this, and
> hence comes a large part of their current unrest, their unhappi-
> ness and their mood of anxiety. And now it is to be expected that
> the other of the two 'Heavenly Powers,' eternal Eros, will make
> an effort to assert himself in the struggle with his equally immor-
> tal adversary.   (p. 145)

Here Freud's seraphs, as powerful and as mortally dangerous as Rilke's angels, are locked eternally in mortal combat. With the encounter of Love-and-Death in our city, and with a distant sound of a trumpet that might cry hope to us all, more needed now even than when Freud was writing thirty years ago, he ends his vision.

IV

Behind Freud, Novalis, says Norman Brown; behind Wagner, Novalis, says Thomas Mann; "the ardent and holy Novalis" Emerson calls him; as early as the 1820's Carlyle was calling us to pay attention to this young German poet, twenty-eight when he died, in a long essay on him with translated excerpts from his works. Still almost no one, outside of Germany and apart from the literary historians who docket and dispose of him amongst the Early Romantics, knows anything about him, perhaps not even his name, and his works are still very hard to come by in English translation. He must therefore have some introduction here.

Novalis, or Friedrich von Hardenberg which was his real name, lived from 1772 to 1801. Of an aristocratic pious family in Thuringia, he survived childhood as many of his brothers and sisters did not, to grow up into a brilliant and lively being, good to look at—so his friend Ludwig Tieck tells us. His studies at various universities centred first on law, later on mining, but were very wide-ranging, including mathematics, sciences, and philosophy under Fichte; besides Fichte and Tieck Novalis was acquainted or friendly with Schiller, Friedrich Schlegel and Schelling. His mind settled into seeing the possibility of some great synthesis of the disciplines, all of which interested him including politics and religion, with poetry at the heart of it. The *Fragmente* are his notes on all these interests. He also left the first part of an unfinished novel on the poetic vocation, *Heinrich von Ofterdingen;* the fragment, *Die Lehrlinge zu Sais,* which is an allegory of the life of heuristic; various minor prose works; and a number of poems, among them the *Hymnen an die Nacht,* the Hymns to the Night which we shall be concerned with. He succumbed to the consumption which had decimated his family at the age of twenty-eight.

Had Novalis himself been telling you his life-story, however, he would not have said anything like this. I think he would have said first, "I loved Sophie and she died." If ever there was a life haunted, or irradiated, by love-and-death, his is that life.

In *Die Lehrlinge zu Sais* each apprentice at the temple has his own special method in the work of interpreting the world. The "I" of the story, clumsier and more groping than the others, has chosen as his special key the love between man and woman. This clue enters the novel also, in Heinrich's love for Mathilde, and Eros plays a central part in the interpolated fairy-tale, *Klingsohrs Märchen,* and, figuratively, in everything Novalis wrote, for he writes of erotic love with an uncompulsive openness and friendliness unlike anyone else in modern times, seeing no reason to keep love and sex separate from his deeply-loved and simply-held Christian beliefs; the whole refreshing beyond words.

Eros met Novalis first, as far as we know, in Leipzig in 1792, and Novalis felt him to be a fierce master to judge by his comments at the time. The great love of his life was to begin two years later when he first met Sophie von Kühn. She was twelve years of age. In the autumn of the year following he became engaged to her. She had already that summer had one bout of serious illness; in 1796 she had an operation in Jena. By now Novalis' closest and dearest brother, Erasmus, was also gravely ill, and during these months Novalis watched both of them moving towards death, Sophie dying in March, 1797, aged fifteen, Erasmus a month later at the age of twenty-three. Sophie's death gave rise in Novalis to a decision, conscious and often repeated to himself and meditated on, as can be seen from the diary he kept at this time: the decision not to live. There was no question for him of suicide; he had just decided against life and for death. It did not affect his living nor his activity, professional and literary, though his friends saw it in him and commented on it, feeling as if he had gone over to another world already. He was busy, lived and worked normally, and in 1798 he met Julie von Charpentier and became engaged to her. Nearly all of his best work dated from this time, but by 1800 he was already seriously ill with hemorrhages. Early in 1801 he was taken home to his father's house where Julie went to nurse him. He did not seem to know that he was dying, all went so quietly, while those who watched by him, his friends Schlegel and Tieck among them, on his last day, March 25, 1801, scarcely knew when he was gone, from his sweet and untroubled face.

To some, Novalis is a beloved friend as he was to Tieck, who says of him in a memoir that he can only marvel at and love his breadth of learning, philosophical genius and gifts as a poet. To others, there may well be much in his life that is shocking: the second engagement comparatively soon after the death of his Sophie; the decision for death; the youthfulness of his beloved and the way in which he exalts her, after her death, into a kind of key to mysteries in this life and the next.

The first point of question, conventional proprieties apart which are never the concern of poets, is in fact interesting evidence of Novalis' essential health. A life so penetrated with love-and-death may conjure up before us visions of emotional melancholia, whereas the subject in question proves a great deal more robust than our nice sensibilities allow. The second love disqualifies neither the first nor the resolution about death. It simply holds love-and-death and life together. A real devotion to love-and-death in this heart needed no external validation of conforming gestures. It was too much a part of life.

The second, the resolve to die, is less easy to explain—not in itself but because it may be understood only by those who are capable, at least in some degree, of an absolute love. This very capability may familiarize such a being early with suffering, from which comes a certain indifference to death or, to put it the other way, to life. Novalis speaks in a letter from Leipzig to his father, already in 1793, of "a certain indifference to life, which will seem a paradox to you because you don't know all of me. I am firmly convinced that there are worse losses in this world than loss of life ... and that life must always be only a means and almost never an end in itself, and that one often loses little when one takes leave of this star of ours." Those who know this turn of thought, in themselves or in friends, will know it to be neither gloomy nor morbid. Those who do not are probably not going to understand it anyway. This is the first stage of it. The second, which Novalis shows forth after 1797, is known to those who in an absolute love have met death, in one of its several forms. Then, in the balance of indifference in the heart between life and death, the scale dips right down towards death, and remains there. Hearts like these desire death. They know, behind a perfectly normal and active life, that, as St. Paul says, "To depart is far better." It is not at all a longing for consolation in an after-life, though as perhaps Novalis shows, the longing not for the hereafter but for death can only be entertained unscathed in a Christian context, for reasons, however, other than those of a promise of personal immortality. All that matters here is that it should be seen, if possible, as a perfectly comprehensible and rational human bent.

There remains the third—the extreme youth of Sophie when Novalis falls so passionately but patiently in love with her, and the incongruity of a young thing scarcely out of the schoolroom becoming after her death in her poet-lover's thoughts a clue, not merely particular but somehow representative and general, to certain deep mysteries of man and universe. Yet this is no new thing . . . "she appeared to me at the beginning of her ninth year almost, and I saw her almost at the end of my ninth year . . . At that moment, I say most truly that the spirit of life which hath its dwelling in the secretest chamber of the heart, began to tremble so violently that the least pulses of my body shook therewith . . . I say that, from that time forward, Love quite governed my soul." *Hic incipit Vita Nova*—Dante wrote it, it is thought, before he was thirty, when his beloved was already dead so that we find him saying, "Death, I hold thee passing good / Henceforth, and a most gentle sweet relief, / Since my dear love has chosen to dwell with thee." We know to what heights he later exalted her. If we are going to be shocked at Novalis at this point, we shall have to be shocked at Dante too; and that seems a work of supererogation.

Auden, we recall, compared Freud to Dante in his epic journey through the underworld among the lost and the damned. It is Ludwig Tieck, fellow-author and friend, who compares Novalis to Dante under a different aspect: "among the moderns he resembles solely and uniquely the sublime Dante, and sings to us, as he did, an unfathomable and mystic song." 'Mystic'—there is that dangerous word again, closing off this central research of Western poetry so as to make it seem esoteric and exceptional instead of what it is—one of the great highways of thought and work in the poetic dynasty on behalf of our culture. The point of work is to explore and maintain the relation between human love-and-death, including the erotic, with the love and death of God in the Christian story.

Poets, and saints, are about the only people nowadays who are not upset by this conjunction. Our alarm is a symptom of the split between these two which is accepted now as practically absolute. Our labelling the poets' attempts to join them up 'mysticism' is in fact to try to keep them separate, for by 'mystical' we know, if we are honest, that we mean something that has no reference at all to ordinary sane human lives. Alternatively, we can be shocked at what they are doing, recoiling from it that way. The split seems to be one of the results of that great fission of Christendom we call the Reformation, for from then onwards Christianity on either side of the fissure seems to have shut itself off by a *cordon sanitaire* from the erotic. Think of the poets who have been at work on uniting the two even during the last hundred years—Baudelaire, Coventry Patmore,[8] Wagner, Rimbaud, Claudel perhaps—and you will realize how many of them have been dubbed mystical or shocking or both. Yet Dante saw in this a matter for his life-work, and Chaucer takes it serenely and largely forward in his greatest poems. Here Tieck's comparison of Novalis to Dante is illuminating, for we owe the renewal of this centuries-old aspect of the work of the poetic dynasty to two poets in the main. Novalis is one; the other is Blake. Only in this context are we going to understand at all what the *Hymnen an die Nacht* are seeking to do, those seven hymns in their strange, groping, ecstatic metre which assert with a great passion the unity and significance of man and woman in love-and-death and in the end bring both home to God.

Novalis began these sacred songs soon after Sophie's death in 1797, and they were completed and published two years later. They

---

[8] It is one of the great ironies that Patmore was induced to destroy his principal work on this theme, *Sponsa Dei*, because of the shocked disapproval of another much less central religious poet, Gerard Manley Hopkins.

are not sharply divided by formal breaks or individual titles, and form a sequence of two groups, the first four and the last three. The form comments on the gentle progression of the subject matter from images for human love-and-death into the synthesis of these in the life, suffering and resurrection of Christ, and in the course of this the verse-form changes from irregularity into the rhymed and definite shape of a hymn in the more orthodox sense, a church chorale. They are held to be among the most beautiful poems in the German language, and that is partly why I give, in the Appendix, the original text of the passages I have translated. (A word, since unhappily our divisions make this necessary, about Novalis' Church loyalties. His family belonged to the Herrnhuter or Moravians, and he was brought up in that strict, pious, evangelical tradition which emphasized prayer and devotion to the person of Christ. These are the notes to be heard in the *Geistliche Lieder,* but so far was the poet from all sectarianism that his short essay of 1799, *Die Christenheit oder Europa,* scandalized his Protestant contemporaries by looking forward to some wide spiritual reuniting of Europe in a truly catholic Christianity, a vision Christians are just beginning to yearn towards 170 years later. Thus do the poets outstrip us.)

It is characteristic of Novalis' spirit that he should begin his first Hymn to Night with thirty-five lines in praise of Light, as king over all the detailed marvels and metamorphoses of the earth, from the fiery sun to the poet's singing mouth. From this the poet gently turns away, to invoke the Night under a dark, sacred, human form. With Night come all the stars, shining out not just in the night sky but within the soul:

> The eyes without number
> Which the Night
> Has opened in us.
> Their gaze goes farther
> Than the very faintest
> Of the countless star-host.
> Having need of no light,
> They see down to the deeps
> Of a love-living spirit . . .

And in this dark and out of this world the beloved comes in the

Night which is sacred to love, and the Hymn ends in the consumma-
tion of love on Night's altar and bride-bed.

The second tells of Sleep, which, like death, is not a mere incident and break in living, but pervades all life. It is in the golden
liquor of grapes, the oil from the almond, the poppy's brown juice,
and gives its charm to the young girl's breast and body. (Novalis
joins Freud and Ortega in commenting on the strange likeness between Eros and Hypnos.) We are ignorant about Sleep,

> Having no inkling
> That out of old stories
> You, heaven-opener, come towards us
> And carry the key
> To the dwellings of the blessed ones,
> Of infinite secrets
> The silent speaker.

In the third, sorrow at the beloved's death is transformed in a moment of illumination when the fetter of light and the bond of birth
are broken, and sorrow flows together to make a new unfathomable
world, where, in a dream, the poet meets his dead love.

The fourth leads into this new world. There is water, first; who-
ever has wet his lips in this water, imperceptible to our common
senses, which springs deep in the hill or grave-mound at whose foot
the external waters of the world go breaking,

> Who has stood up there
> On this boundary-range of the world,
> Looked over and down to the unknown land,
> Where Night inhabits,
> Truly, he turns not back
> To the busying world again,
> To the land
> Where light is ruler
> And turmoil ever at home.
> Up there he builds him a hutment,
> Hutment of quiet,
> And he longs
> And loves
> And gazes over,

> Till the welcomest hour of them all
> Draws him down into the waterspring's fountain.

In that water all that is earthly is cast up as foam and brims over
and is lost,

> But all that the touch
> Of love made holy
> Runs flowing and free in secretive channels
> Through that other country,
> Where it,
> Cloud-like,
> Mingles with slumbering Loves.

This is the landscape-of-the-other, of love-and-death, which Rilke
too opened to us in the Tenth Elegy; yet is it not also the stream
which Wordsworth and Coleridge knew, the underground stream
which is thought (for body and mind and world are not separate,
and living and dead conjoin here in a living stream where the ancestral voices and the ghostly echoes of the ancient earth are)?

In the fifth Hymn the poet draws a new breath. We move from
the celebration of love-and-death in human terms to their meaning
in the divine, and the change of direction is again introduced by a
hymn to Light, which is also an affirmation of life and the day's
work. Following this, the poet passes on now to myth and to religion. Novalis depicts at the beginning the lovely world of ancient
myth, anthropomorphic through and through, its beauty marred by
only one thought, "Nur *ein* Gedanke wars" which could not be fitted
into this world, by priest or lover or poet—the thought of Death.
(Here the pattern of the verse changes, and three solemn eight-line
stanzas are inset.) Gradually this old world dies, and nature waits,
cold and lifeless, till the new life appears. A birth is recounted, simple, poor, in a night star-bedecked—and we realize the poet is telling
the story of Christ. He appears first as Love:

> Lonely unfolded
> That heart out of heaven
> To the blaze
> And bosom of Love,
> Turned to the Father's lofty countenance . . .

Then comes a singer from Greece to Palestine (how like Hölderlin this is!) who, in that earlier solemn verse-form, sings the newcomer, but as Death:

> Thou art the youth whom we have everywhere
> Carved on our grave-stones, sunk in meditation—
> A sign of comfort in the darkened air,
> Of nobler men the bright initiation;
> What sank us once in uttermost despair
> Seems to us sweetly now an invitation.
> In death was endless life announced the soul—
> For thou art Death; now first thou mak'st us whole.

In the poem Christ moves now straight to His death, and with this a new world is born where we all belong

> In the kingdom of Love
> And we serve in the temple
> Of the heavenly Death.

Our own death is a call to a wedding, "Zur Hochzeit ruft der Tod," as it runs in the formal stanzas ending this hymn, a thought marvellously elaborated in the Song of the Dead found among Novalis' papers as part of his unfinished novel, but here the Biblical figure, the marriage feast of the Lamb, visualized as a great sea of light, joy, golden wine, an eternal poem, a night of love transformed by the sun of God's countenance into some single united never-ending glory. We began these Hymns with earthly light, we end with a heavenly, and it is the longing for this, and its realization in the person of Christ, which the seventh Hymn sounds. Christ Himself is spoken of in terms which gather together note after note of what we have been thinking of, He who in the glow of youth made Himself known to us as God, the poet says, and devoted His life to an early death in a passion of love, making Himself no stranger to fear and suffering if so be He might thereby gain and hold our love.

Novalis in the *Hymnen an die Nacht* has hold of two things. First, like Rilke and Freud, he holds to the central importance of love-and-death in intimate connection, not only in the human life but as a figure with interpretative power. Secondly, he divines that

Christianity is accessible under this figure and that it has a marvellous treasure at its disposal at this point, in the life of its Founder, in the figures which it has chosen to employ (for Novalis' figures in these last Hymns are Biblical, not invented), and in the answering lives of the great dynasty of saints. Of our three poets working at this point of love-and-death towards greater power and vision, he is the one who holds love-and-death and religion together. The other two reject it, Rilke as a suffocating irrelevance to true human life and advance, Freud as a relic of infantilism with which, however, under the form of the Judaeo-Christian religion, he wrestles all his life, as Rilke also does, rather differently, in his turn. We shall misunderstand here if we see these three poets as two unbelievers and one *bien-pensant*. The two more modern poets see clearly the results of that split we spoke of earlier; upon Christianity which has for centuries now hoarded up its treasure as if behind safe strong walls of an ingrowing theology and a defensive attitude to the world instead of squandering it abroad for the relief of the needy; and upon everyman who now goes pursuing something he calls "love" in an ever-growing desperation of devalued carnality. It is because of the urgency of our situation that Novalis' answer, in its human realism, is so important.

In this way love-and-death, like heroic suffering and virtue, becomes not merely a passing human experience but a place where work is to be done towards further advance. Rilke says that we must in our individual lives remake the erotic into the human by reconnecting it with death, and death with love, and that this will in turn reshape our communal works and lives; Freud says that we must learn to struggle with and against these two vast antipathetic powers in our material, psychic and civil existence; Novalis says that we shall enter fully into love-and-death only if we draw out of our religion the key which it holds at this point. Thus, as with the suffering and effort which we were looking at previously, what seem to be simple near-physical phenomena of individual human lives can become working points, figures by which we may understand our troubled present, and prefigure in suffering and effort and love and death some way towards that more fully human future to which all poetry looks.

Epilogue

THE WHOLE OF MAN'S OPERATION, NO MATTER HOW HE TRIES
to divide it up into various spheres for reasons of intellectual
or practical convenience, is one and the same. We began by thinking about the work that has to go on all the time upon man himself, individually and communally: the extending of his power and
knowledge, and the creating of his image of himself by means of,
and in terms of, his methods of thought. Besides being everyman's
necessary work, this is also the united concern of those seven in-
quiring and constructing dynasties of ours.

The work does not go on somewhere in a no-man's-land of
theory, but wherever men think and talk and read about matters
above the level of sheer animal existence, and are ready to make
and be made. One would hope that might describe the classroom,
in school or university; and since education is clearly deeply involved with this work, and mental activity and openness to change
are rather more likely to be found amongst the young, we took a
particular group, students in the United States, as a kind of index
and diagnostic of the state of this great over-all work in the present
time.

There emerged what was on the whole a negative picture, in
terms of abstraction and the loss of a living imaginative relation
with the natural universe, producing conditions of hunger and fear.

The deprivation is apparent among the young in the academic world but there are echoes of something similar, in life-forms if not immediately in thought-forms, among young people everywhere. Nor is it simply a matter of today, as we can see from warnings uttered by poets a long time ago now. In the uneasy image man has made for himself, half abstraction, half machine, there seemed to be a resemblance to the method of thought we have pursued in the West for three hundred years, one which still holds undisputed sway in the modern world. This method pursues one form of thought exclusively, that of operation with abstract analytic mathematical figures which are then extended and embodied in the operations of technology. From this method our current image of ourselves is made.

This is not—it cannot be too often repeated for there has been much misunderstanding hereabouts—to belittle or deny the power and beauty of mathematical figuring. Poets tend to have a passion for pure forms, of which this type of thought is a close approximation, and which are an essential part of the poet's art and manner of seeing. It is simply to indicate what happens when one type of figuring excludes any other. Poetry knows of such another and has to exhibit it. This method calls in consciously the whole figure of the human organism of mind and body, fuses it with its own instrument of language, and from this builds up its thought in an organic and human frame by which the human being and his universe are to be related and interpreted. This is what I have been calling the human metaphor. I could equally well have called it poetry. Poets perhaps more than any other dynasty are deeply concerned with mastering and communicating this method, in their own thinking, their work and their lives, all of which hold together. This is one of the reasons why poetry is to so great an extent a public and a teaching discipline, so that poets are always straying over into education.

There used to be three sources from which this form of thought could be learned, it seems to me, and where it could be practised at different levels available to everybody. The three are metaphysics, poetry and religion. To name them is to indicate once again why we suffer loss at present: we have lost them all. Philosophy, even in so far as it remains a feature of education or of our intellectual life, has proscribed metaphysics. Poetry is nowhere. And if we are going to be honest we shall admit that religion as a real shaping force in education or in life has been thrust out more or less totally. The restoration of all three in whatever renewed and shining shapes are needed, and their reunion with the great tradition of mathematics and science to create man's full method and with it his full image—perhaps these will come out of the hunger and fear of the young as things are now.

This is part of the poet's business. One after another of the poets has recognized the need and imagined its fulfilment; Newman in *The Idea of a University;* Shelley in *A Defence of Poetry* ("We want the creative faculty to imagine that which we know[1]; we want the generous impulse to act that which we imagine; we want the poetry of life: our calculations have outrun conception; we have eaten more than we can digest") and in *Prometheus Unbound;* and Blake. Already in our first Chapter we glanced at this prophet's recognition of our trouble, as he figures it in *Jerusalem,* and at one aspect of his final vision of synthesis in the last six Chapters of the poem, when to the clangor of the Arrows of Intellect the great union is made in Heaven between the scientific analytic forms of thought on the one hand and the poetic forms on the other. Image after image, of those we have been looking at in our study, meet in this seeing of Blake's:

> Jesus said: "Wouldst thou love one who never died
> "For thee, or ever die for one who had not died for thee?
> "And if God dieth not for Man and giveth not himself
> "Eternally for Man, Man could not exist; for Man is Love
> "As God is Love: every kindness to another is a little Death
> "In the Divine Image, nor can Man exist but by Brother-
> hood . . ."

> Albion . . . threw himself into the furnaces of affliction.
> All was a Vision, all a Dream: the Furnaces became

[1] "To imagine that which we know"—*imaginare quicquid cognitum* in the Latin into which Mr. Joseph Morello put it—a marvellous device or watchword for any place of learning.

> Fountains of Living Waters flowing from the Humanity
> Divine.
> And all the Cities of Albion rose from their Slumbers . . .
>
> 　　　　　　　　　　　　. . . so spake in my hearing
> The Universal Father. Then Albion stretch'd his hand into
> Infinitude
> And took his bow . . .
> And the Bow is a Male and Female, and the Quiver of the
> Arrows of Love
> Are the Children of this Bow, a Bow of Mercy and Loving
> Kindness laying
> Open the hidden Heart in Wars of mutual Benevolence,
> Wars of Love,
> And the Hand of Man grasps firm between the male and
> female Loves.
> And he clothed himself in Bow and Arrows, in awful state,
> Fourfold,
> In the midst of his Twenty-eight Cities, each with his Bow
> breathing.

It is to mutilate Blake's vision to quote him piecemeal like this; but read the whole, and you will discover that the Arrows of Love that clothe man here, and the Arrows of Intellect whose unloosing accompanies the marriage of man's two great methods, analysis and poetry, are one and the same. The integrity of the organism is restored before the face of God, while Death, the poet says, becomes "regenerations terrific" according to "the wonders Divine of Human Imagination," in which, for the poet, all human endeavours meet.

We miss the whole point if we see this, along with other such visions of the poets, as apocalyptic dreaming and no more. It is a programme of education. Milton, most fittingly in his treatise on Education, seems to challenge us to apprehend, truly and almost as if for the first time, "what religious, what glorious and magnificent use might be made of Poetry both in divine and human things." Of this the human metaphor is a part, revealing, in Blake's no less quintessential words, the Lineaments of Man.

Appendix

THE FOLLOWING ARE THE GERMAN TEXTS OF PASSAGES
quoted in Chapter Five, Section IV, from *Hymnen an die Nacht* by
Novalis.

. . . die unendlichen Augen,
Die die Nacht
In uns geöffnet.
Weiter sehn sie
Als die blässesten
Jener zahllosen Heere.
Unbedürftig des Lichts
Durchschaun sie die Tiefen
Eines liebenden Gemüts . . .

Ahnden nicht,
Dass aus alten Geschichten
Du himmelöffnend entgegentrittst
Und den Schlüssel trägst
Zu den Wohnungen der Seligen,
Unendlicher Geheimnisse
Schweigender Bote.

Wer oben stand
Auf diesem Grenzgebürge der Welt
Und hinübersah in das neue Land,
Wahrlich, der kehrt nicht

In das Treiben der Welt zurück,
Wo das Licht regiert
Und ewige Unruh haust.
Oben baut er sich Hütten,
Hütten des Friedens,
Sehnt sich
Und liebt,
Schaut hinüber,
Bis die willkommenste aller Stunden
Hinunter ihn in den Brunnen der Quelle zieht.

Aber was heilig ward
Durch der Liebe Berührung,
Rinnt aufgelöst in verborgenen Gängen
Auf das jenseitige Gebiet,
Wo es,
Wie Wolken,
Sich mit entschlummerten Lieben mischt.

Einsam entfaltete
Das himmlische Herz sich
Zu der Liebe
Glühendem Schoss,
Des Vaters hohem Antlitz zugewandt . . .

Der Jüngling bist du, der seit langer Zeit
Auf unsern Gräbern steht in tiefen Sinnen—
Ein tröstlich Zeichen in der Dunkelheit,
Der höhern Menschen freudiges Beginnen;
Was uns gesenkt in tiefe Traurigkeit,
Zieht uns mit süsser Sehnsucht nun von hinnen.
Im Tode ward das ewge Leben kund—
Du bist der Tod und machst uns erst gesund.

. . . Im Reiche der Liebe
Und dienen im Tempel
Des himmlischen Todes.

Index